WARRINGTON ACADEMY
1757-86
ITS PREDECESSORS AND SUCCESSORS

By P. O'Brien, M.D.

ISBN 0 9514333 0 X

First published February 1989

Designed, produced and published by
Owl Books,
P.O.Box 60,
Wigan, Lancashire WN1 2QB

Printed and bound in England

Ad Majoram Dei Gloriam

FOREWORD

When I came to Warrington in the early summer of 1981 to fight what turned out to be quite a famous bye-election, I did not know the town at all. Indeed I remember being rather mocked for implying in an early television interview that it was in Lancashire not Cheshire. This I did not regard as a solecism, for I was loath to recognize the presumptuous county boundary changes which were then only seven years old. In historical terms I instinctively thought of it as the southernmost bastion of the Lancashire industrial area, and having in addition the quality, which it shared with Wigan and Preston, of being astride the great westerly route to Scotland, as well as being the median point between the metropolitan cities of Liverpool and Manchester, and almost the last point before the Mersey became estuarial.

In other words, I thought of Warrington as being a meeting point as well as a manufacturing town. What I did not expect was a place with a feel of history. I quickly came to realise that I was wrong. I was almost immediately struck by the tight-knit quality of the town, the relative stability of its population as well as its industries, and the same roots going back to and beyond the beginnings of the industrial revolution. Later, it did not in the least surprise me to discover that it had a vigorous Literary and Philosophical Society, founded in 1870, devoted to the history of the town as well as to wider intellectual interests, with which I once spent a most rewarding evening.

Dr Paddy O'Brien as a historian is a product of that Society, and a very notable one. He has unlocked for me, with scholarship, style and verve, a third level of knowledge about Warrington and a whole educational movement. In the third quarter of the eighteenth century Warrington came nearer to being the third university city of England than had done anywhere else, except for Stamford in the early fourteenth century, between 1200 and 1830. Warrington Academy, "the still-born university" as he calls it with a combination of medical and historical insight, had distinguished alumni, rather good buildings, a wide curriculum, and very nearly made a major break-through. But, alas, it was short-lived, surviving only 26 years, although some of its traditions migrated to Manchester, and then, bringing in a tributary from York, to London, before settling in the 1890's foundation of Manchester College, Oxford.

Particularly when associated with Warrington, movements which nearly made a major break-through have a special fascination for me. But I think that, even without this individual connection, I would have found Dr O'Brien's book rewarding and enjoyable. He has a good subject in territory which has been unworked since 1943, and he exploits it with skill and sympathy.

Roy Jenkins

ACKNOWLEDGEMENTS

I am indebted to many people for assistance in bringing this work forward, starting with librarians, who are ever the mainstay of such endeavour. We are most fortunate in Warrington to have an incomparable Local History library, which owes its origin to the staff and associates of Warrington Academy. Dave Rodgers, the librarian, has cheerfully given much time, assistance and advice over several years; members of his staff have been helpful and courteous at all times. The librarians at Dr Williams' and Manchester College, Oxford, have helped on several occasions, as have Charles Parrish and Margaret Norwell of Newcastle Lit. & Phil. Society, and A. L. Smyth of the Manchester Society; also, Christine Strickland of Kendal library and Rev. Fr M. Sharratt of Ushaw College, Durham. Warrington Museum has given me access to the Barbauld medallion, and BNFL has provided inspiration in commissioning a model of the long since demolished premises in Academy Place. David Henderson, principal of Priestley College, gave me permission to photograph the statue of Joseph Priestley. Dan Doherty lent me his fine copy of the 1826 map.

Rev. Dr John McLachlan gave permission to draw extensively on his father's writing and has discussed the project from time to time. Rev. Dr G. F. Nuttall, late of New College, London, has read the proofs and given much useful advice. My friend Dr Ian Sellers, late of Padgate College, as a well versed ecclesiastical historian has made useful contribution and comment. Professor Bill McCarthy of Iowa State University spent much of 1988 in England studying the works of Mrs Barbauld; we have exchanged much material over the past year and given each other mutual support. Rev. Dewi E. Davies of Aberystwyth College has provided information on the Carmarthen succesion. My friend Dr Fred Miller, lecturer in the History of Medicine at Newcastle, has advised on that special topic. My old school mate Prof. F. X. Martin of University College, Dublin, has discussed England's "hedge schools" with me.

On the production side, my word processor Jen Darling has worked long and hard, assisted by her husband Chris who is a mine of technical know-how; their combination begat perfection in the typescript. My publisher, Alan Roby, has stimulated me with his enthusiasm and expertise, assisted by Josie, his wife, who has been helpful throughout. My own wife, Sheila, has provided encouragement and support, with much forbearance.

Conant Brodribb of Oxford and Lady Betsy Rodgers of Kent, who have been helpful with information and advice, are descendants of the Aikins. Among many others who have helped are: Robert Oxley of Penketh; Malcolm Deacon of Northampton, author of a recent biography of Philip Doddridge; Miss M. Massey, secretary of Cairo Street chapel, and Rev. Eric Wild, a former minister there; Harold Wright of Market Harborough, and Miss Betty Ward of Kibworth; Rev. K. L. Lee and K. L. Gillott of Daventry; Rev. E. J. R. Cook of Cross Street chapel, Manchester; Rev. G. Jones of the Kendal chapel, Dr J. Satchell of Kendal Civic Society, and Winifred Inglesfield of Natland.

GUIDE TO THE CHARTS

The charts are an essential element in this study for any who wish to understand the development portrayed in its full perspective. In anatomical terms they are akin to an x-ray study which reveals not only the bones, but how they lie and how well they articulate.

The facts are presented in considerable detail which will be of interest to more specialised readers, but it is the broad patterns emerging which are of particular significance. The Cross Street chapel study shows this most clearly in its relationships with the group of northern academies through to Manchester College. The Warrington chapel has a mixed relationship, with the potent entry of the Midlands group. Kibworth chapel relates backwards to the northern group and forwards to the successors of Kibworth Academy at Northampton, Daventry and on to Warrington. The Kibworth family study reflects the same connections, in another light. Finally the academies chart demonstrates the close relationship that develops between these two groups in the north and the Midlands.

In terms of biological evolution they also reveal mutations. It has been noted that Jollie's Academy at Attercliffe is seen as something of an aberration. The same might well be said of Manchester College at York; this can be seen as a sort of spiritual retreat which gave the establishment new strength, but it also took it out of the mainstream of academic growth.

Had the college remined at Manchester in the early decades of the 19th century it would have coincided with the birth of the first new universities at Durham and London, and would therefore have been firmly poised as the focus for Manchester University well before Owen's College came on the scene.

Moving to a geographical analogy Manchester College could have been a powerful headwater to this mainstream of academic development, instead of which it became a quiet backwater of the Isis, lapping the base of ivory towers.

INTRODUCTION

'. . . if we lower our standard in History, we cannot uphold it in church or state.'

Lord Acton

Approaching the story of England's non-conformist academies for the first time the reader is likely to be thoroughly confused by the complicated ecclesiastical and legal issues involved. The initial chapter attempts to unravel these and to set them out as simply as possible.

The main aim of this work is to consider one group of these academies, and successor colleges with a particular tradition, and in doing so to outline and explore a pattern of succession and development which has been considered in the past, but with differing conclusions. This particular group established a tradition of liberal education which was to have a powerful influence at the advent of the new 'red brick universities' in the 19th century.

Warrington and Manchester are central to this story, but Warrington was the high point and so its Academy is dealt with at greater length than any of the other establishments. Much stress is laid on its social life, because this is an important factor in the vibrant nature of that foundation in its heyday; also, sadly, in its eventual downfall. The more detailed chapters carry the account of a few individuals well beyond their narrower involvement with particular academies. This is justified to the extent that their careers throw further light on the cultural and educational milieu which gave them inspiration. Also, a detailed study of one establishment tells us much about the movement as a whole.

Warrington is less well known than Manchester as a place with a cultural background, but it is an ancient town with roots in national, ecclesiastical, educational and cultural history which go back long before the advent of the non-conformist academies. A few relevant facts are presented to put this in context. It is hoped that this presentation will bring alive again for the town's people the exciting story of its long defunct Academy, together with its wider connections and its leading role in an important national movement destined to revitalise higher education.

For the U.S.A. the story is also relevant because this alternative tradition in British eduction provided inspiration for new colleges and universities which were being established, even before the umbilical cord was cut.

All of this has been told before and in much greater detail, so what justification can there be for a new book? It is that the details are scattered through many different works, some contemporary with the academies and some more recent, but all now out of print and only available to those prepared to hunt in specialist libraries. Also there has been the challenge of exploring certain issues from new angles, which will always occur with time. Some of these are contentious and may not win unanimous approbation, as for instance the thorny question of succession, but they have been interesting to pursue, and should stimulate others to consider the issues again.

The author believes that the charts, which have been drawn to illustrate this work, throw a clearer light on the connections between a particular group of academies, as well as between these academies and the ministers of certain chapels; and also with certain closely knit family groups, which parallel the academies in their connections. At the same time other individuals shoot off at a tangent or come in on a tangent to establish links with the broad pattern of the Dissenter academies as a whole. It is difficult for a reader approaching this subject for the first time to grasp the detailed web of connections from text alone, and so it is hoped that the charts will simplify the effort. Joseph Priestley, who pioneered this approach, with his charts of biography and history, would no doubt approve.

In 1986 Manchester College, Oxford, celebrated the bicentenary of its establishment as Manchester Academy, but it also acknowledges its roots in Warrington, whose Academy was dissolved in the same year, and whose library and archives it still preserves. In Warrington the bicentenary was marked with an exhibition in the local library, which itself has roots in the Academy. The present work is fruit of the research which lay behind that exhibition and of many years of reading and exploration on the ground.

The terms Dissenter and Non-Conformist are treated for practical purposes as interchangeable, although there are subtle differences. However, those who fail to conform will usually do so because they dissent. At least this will be so if their stance is rational and conscientious.

CONTENTS

Warrington 1783, from South bank of Mersey at Latchford. Parish church of St. Elphin's at East end. Holy Trinity church West of riverside buildings, old St. James' at Latchford near southern end of the bridge which is obscured by trees. Academy Place is behind the mill and Sankey Street chapel just West of Holy Trinity.

Chapter 1
REFORMATION, REVOLUTION AND CIVIL STRIFE

'You've got to be taught
Before it's too late
Before you are six or seven or eight
To hate all the people your relatives hate
You've got to be carefully taught!'
'South Pacific' – Rodgers and Hammerstein

The history of the non-conformist academies is rooted in the nation's religious upheavals from Henry VIII onwards. The Reformation in England followed a different course from that on the continent, and it is essential to explore these variations to understand what followed.

England, like its neighbouring island, might well have remained an outpost of Roman Catholicism were it not for Henry's domestic and dynastic problems. In the early days of his reign the King had been a darling of the Papacy, favoured with the title, 'Defender of the Faith', which the monarchy still holds dear. The relationship only soured when Henry found his wishes for annulment of his marriage frustrated by Rome. He believed there was plenty of precedent for such an accommodation, especially for such an influential and favoured ruler as himself. His lust for a new and attractive young queen, who might bear him a son, would brook no delay, but Rome proved obdurate and the King lost patience.

His solution was to nationalise the Church, though he never saw it as other than 'The Catholic Church' with an Anglican instead of a Roman head. He had little enthusiasm for theological reformation. But, movements which start with a limited objective have a habit of escalating, and various of Henry's subjects had their own reasons for promoting further change. Having put the church under his own royal command, reformers were quick to stress abuses in the clerical establishment. The Church, and especially many of its great monasteries, were possessed of enormous wealth, and it was well known that there were many instances of abuse, both material and moral.

Henry's Chancellor **Wolsey** knew these flaws, and had plans for internal reformation and reorganisation of the establishments most affected. But he himself fell into disfavour when the King's matrimonial cause faltered, and his enthusiasm for promoting it came into question. Others around the court, soon to be led by **Thomas Cromwell**, were quick to detect great potential in the schemes on which Wolsey had been working; not only could the church be reformed for its own benefit, but if religious houses were suppressed their wealth need not necessarily remain with the Church to redistribute among its more worthy sections. Here indeed was a goldmine, which could be a wonderful source of royal patronage, and the grateful beneficiaries would have a strong incentive for ensuring that there should be no return to Rome's domination.

This was the action which did most to ensure success for English reformers; but it was very much a negative aspect of reform. There were others around, with different motives, who were excited by the direction in which religious development was moving on the continent, which was much more positively theological.

Today, there are few on any side who would deny that great abuses were corrupting post-medieval Christianity, so that reform was both essential and urgent. As with any organisation in crisis they soon divided into those who would reform from within and those who saw the whole structure as so corrupt that only a clean break and a fresh start would achieve their objectives. Internal reformers had their successes, but soon the leadership became ultra-defensive and reactionary. They have made more progress in the twentieth century than at any time since the break occurred, but still have some way to go.

Those who broke away had two objectives, the reform of church government, and doctrinal reformation. Their models came initially from the thinking and teaching of **Martin Luther** and **John Calvin**. These began to influence English reformers from early on, but at first it was just a small intellectual elite which became involved, although significant movement did occur during the short reign of Edward VI.

When Mary Tudor succeeded to the throne there was a powerful revival of Roman Catholicism, which might have been permanent, were it not for the policies pursued and the methods employed. Instead of exhibiting the Christian virtues of charity and humility Mary's followers entered into a ruthless persecution of committed reformers. Their sin was deemed to be heresy, and the prescribed punishment was burning at the stake. Many good and honest Englishmen suffered in this way, which did nothing to sweeten the temper of people on either side.

With **Elizabeth** it was back to reform and an **Anglican** establishment, and this time it was the Catholics who suffered, but the violence took a different shape. Because of the Pope's action in formally excommunicating the Queen, thus encouraging her overthrow, the crime was now deemed to be treason, and the punishment was the barbarous one of being hung, drawn and quartered.

Many, who had been driven abroad in Mary's time, returned with even greater zeal for reformation, but they were disappointed in Elizabeth's Church of England, which in many ways harked back to that of her father. The Government and Church leaders sought a via media between Rome and Geneva. They accepted the teachings of Calvin, whilst clinging to episcopal control. But the whole concept was Erastian, with Bishops as the Queen's servants, to do as she bade them. The aspirations of the regime were much more in the secular field.

With the advent of the Stuarts, the descendants of Mary Queen of Scots, Protestants were fearful that there might be a slide back to Rome. But the Stuarts were never more than lukewarm about any cause other than their own royal power and how it was to be sustained – preferably by '**Divine Right**'. They were equivocal in their attitude towards, and support for, any Church. They bent easily with the prevailing breeze.

James I showed little regret at leaving behind him the fervour with which John Knox had imbued his native land. His son **Charles**, conservative by nature, supported his reactionary Archbishop of Canterbury, **William Laud**, who aimed at absolutism in Church and State; rooting out Calvinism in England, and its Presbyterian manifestation in Scotland. His fanaticism was so marked that Englishmen abroad were forbidden to attend Calvinist services. Laud favoured elaborate ritual, the doctrine of the 'Real Presence', sacramental confession and celibate clergy. Enforcement would be through the agency of the Star Chamber.

Like most ultra-conservative autocrats neither of these men could gauge the strength and fury of the opposition they provoked. Laud was impeached by the Long Parliament in 1640, on a charge of treason, endeavouring to subvert the laws to overthrow the Protestant religion, and acting as an enemy of Parliament. After a lengthy legal wrangle he was finally beheaded in 1645.

The Archbishop having been removed, the King's own position became much more vulnerable. A precedent had been set which did much to bring about the downfall of Charles himself, and the manner of it. Eventually he too was charged with treason against his people, tried by Parliament, found guilty and beheaded.

In the years which followed, Parliament, backed by the Model Army, was supreme, with **Oliver Cromwell** gradually rising to the position of Supreme Commander, then to be designated Lord

Protector; King in all but name, and even that had been his for the taking. During these years of the Civil War and the Commonwealth the English Revolution was born. Democracy would remain a child for many years to come, until it came of age with the great Reform Act in the nineteenth century. But absolute monarchy was dead, and the great myth of the 'Divine Right of Kings' was buried in the same coffin. By comparison the much trumpeted revolution of 1688 was more of a dynastic shuffle, although it did put a final nail in that coffin.

In religion the **Commonwealth** is remembered as the age of the **Puritans**; the Protestant reformation in England had finally come of age. In retrospect it was also a time of considerable latitude. Church livings were filled with Independents, Presbyterians, a few Baptists, and any Anglicans who could reconcile themselves to the disappearance of Bishops. Cromwell himself favoured the Independents (Congregationalists) and, apart from his ruthless campaign in Ireland, showed a remarkable degree of toleration across the board. In England even Catholics and Quakers enjoyed a brief respite. Not all members of Parliament, nor all officers of the Model Army, were so liberal however. And during the years of the interregnum there was a good deal of strife, promoted by the more extreme puritan groups, whose politics were republican, with a tendency to anarchy at the fringes.

With Cromwell's untimely death, the pretension to royalty was underscored by his followers, who declared that he had nominated his elder son Richard to succeed him, though the evidence for this is rather thin. This succession however was doomed from the start. Richard Cromwell was not another Oliver. England had had enough of being forced into a Puritan straitjacket, and there was a great desire for a return to monarchy. So, after just two years, Charles II was called back.

With the restoration of the Stuarts many false hopes were raised. Roman Catholics had some intermittent expectations of easement right through until James II was defeated by William of Orange at the Boyne. But their time had not come, and it would be more than a century yet before the first Catholic Relief Act, when, in 1778, George III had his back to the wall during the American revolt, and they were prevailed upon humbly to petition him to have the laws changed so that he could use them for cannon fodder.

The Presbyterians had more cause for confidence. The Scottish connection, and recent associations during the Commonwealth, encouraged them to assume royal patronage. So they sent a deputation to Charles in the Netherlands before his restoration had been finally agreed. The upshot of this meeting was the '**Declaration of Breda**' wherein Charles announced: 'We do declare a liberty to tender consciences, and that no man shall be disquieted or called in question for differences of opinion in matters of religion which do not disturb the peace of the kingdom'. But he was reckoning without Parliament, which would allow him no such latitude, a violent anti-Puritan reaction set in, which the newly restored King could not withstand.

The majority in the House of Commons now represented the heirs of Laud, although the Lords were, on the whole, more tolerant. Once again the English Protestant Reformation was on its familiar see-saw, with a violent swing to High Church Episcopalian Anglicanism and no toleration for Dissenters. (No wonder the Vicar of Bray became so canny!)

During the Cromwellian period the Church of England had been heavily infiltrated with Puritan clergy. Now these were obliged to conform or resign. About 2000 of the parish clergy in England and Wales were ejected within two years of the Restoration. The last day for deciding between conformity or ejection was 24 August 1662 - the feast of St. Bartholemew, which is remembered by Dissenters as '**Black Bartholemew**'. But this was not all. The new leaders in Parliament and in the Church were determined to exterminate Non-Conformity root and branch, so the '**Act of Uniformity**' was followed by further harsh repressive legislation referred to collectively as the 'Clarendon Code' or the '**Test Acts**'.

These new laws had dual objectives. The first was to prevent Dissenters coming together for worship. The second was to deprive them of higher education, so that they would be unable to train a new generation of ministers to take over when those recently ejected had passed on. But tyrants and autocrats will never learn the great lesson of history; that harsh repression brings out the finest qualities in people, who react with greater determination than ever to preserve their heritage, even to the point of sacrificing life itself, and short of that they will accept intolerable hardship, privation and loss of esteem outside their own community. At that time, outstanding examples of those prepared to suffer for their beliefs were Richard Baxter and John Bunyan. Others will emerge as the story of the Academies unfolds.

WA—B

Chapter 2
EARLY NON-CONFORMITY AND THE ADVENT OF THE ACADEMIES

'Submit to those who are invested with the supreme power in your country, as your lawful civil magistrates; but if they would prescribe to you in matters of faith, say that you have but one Father even God and one Master even Christ, and stand fast in the liberty with which he has made you free. Respect a parliamentary king, and cheerfully pay all parliamentary taxes; but have nothing to do with a parliamentary religion, or a parliamentary God.'

Joseph Priestley 1772

In 1646 **Robert Yates** was Preacher at Preston, and involved in establishing the Presbyterian classes in that part of Lancashire. Soon after, he removed to Warrington as rector, where it is said he came in 'by the gift and presentation of Gilbert Ireland Esq., the patron, and *the free election of the congregation*.'[1] This shows that not only was the minister himself Presbyterian, but that the congregation he came to serve had elected him.

In 1649 the Presbyterians and Independents were at loggerheads, struggling for mastery within the Cromwellian establishment . The Independents triumphed and marked their victory with an Act of Parliament, by which all persons were required to engage 'to be true and faithful to the Commonwealth as then established, without a king or a House of Lords',[2] which excluded both Royalists and Presbyterians. Yates had such a decided objection to this 'engagement' that he spoke out strongly against it and refused to subscribe to it. For this offence he was arrested and tried at Lancaster. He was convicted and sentenced to death. Determined not to retract, he prepared for execution, writing his last speech and testament, when unexpectedly he was reprieved.[3] He returned to Warrington, and for the remainder of his time as Rector, there were apparently a number of other ministers serving along with him; such was the non-conformist style.

In 1662, after the Restoration, when the new rulers were again bending the clergy to their will with the 'Act of Uniformity', Robert Yates was one of the many who refused to conform, and who was forced to quit his living. Shortly after, he was denounced by enemies under the Five Mile Act and sent to prison again. This Act provided that an ejected minister could not operate within five miles of any town, or of the church in which he had formerly served. Yates, by remaining in the town, would be in default. Thus he suffered under the ruling powers of both sides, who, as Beamont commented, 'could not both be right nor he wrong.'[4] Henry Newcome, the minister who had been ejected from the Collegiate Church (later Cathedral) at Manchester, and other friends, pleaded for Yates and he was released, to continue serving his flock at Warrington under the difficult and hazardous conditions of the time.

In 1672 Charles II again took unilateral action as with the 'Declaration of Breda'. While Parliament was in recess he decided to relax conditions for Dissenters and to issue licences both for preachers and places of worship. Robert Yates obtained a general licence as a Presbyterian preacher, with specific licences permitting him to conduct services at the homes of several of his flock, and in a room or rooms at the court house. This court-house licence is one of the very few from that period still surviving, and is preserved in the town, at the Cairo Street Chapel.[5]

But these licences could not guarantee peace. There was great resentment at the king's leniency, and Yates was violently interrupted while preaching in the courthouse. The following year, when Parliament re-assembled, the King was forced to revoke all the licences that had been issued, thus underlining the very real limitations of his power, and the strong prejudice against non-conformity in the House of Commons, as well as in the Anglican church, which had itself been thoroughly purged of this element.

Persecution was now worse than before. Nathaniel Heywood of Ormskirk commented to a friend, 'Other afflictions are light compared to a dumb mouth and silent sabbaths'. And again, 'I think this turning us out of our licensed places will cost Mr. Yates and myself our lives. Oh, this goes heavily! Our casting out of our great places (1662) was not so much as casting us out of our little places (1672).' Yates died soon after and was succeeded by his son Samuel.[6]

The first objective of the Test Acts, to prevent Dissenters continuing in their own way and coming together for worship, is well illustrated in the life of Robert Yates. The second objective is illustrated in the preparation of his son Samuel to follow in his ministry.[7] Parliament aimed ruthlessly to eradicate dissent by depriving its followers of higher education, to ensure that their ministry would not survive. English parish clergy had for long enough been almost exclusively graduates of Oxford and Cambridge. Now these universities were barred by the Act of Uniformity to any who would not conform.[8]

But, autocratic rulers do not learn from history, as well we know from many examples even in our own time, as in South Africa. People with a cause which they are determined to uphold will choose to suffer great hardship and inconvenience rather than submit to a system which they conscientiously oppose. England already had the example of Catholic recusants who were sacrificing livelihood, estates, even life itself, for their faith, and who had set up seminaries on the continent to educate young men for the priesthood.

English and Welsh dissenters were able to resort to the Scottish Universities where there was no 'Test' to exclude them. There were also establishments on the continent which would serve them. But with great determination they chose a new approach which provided them with a home-made solution. They established academies, mainly to provide a succession of their ministry, but in many cases accommodating young men who wished to enter other professions as well.

These academies were established by men whose prime occupation was ministry to a gathered congregation. In the first generation these were Oxford and Cambridge graduates who had been ejected from the Anglican Church in 1662. They were able scholars who considered themselves fitted, and who felt called upon, to engage in this field of education. The early academies had one tutor and were sited within the minister's own home,[9] which must have thrown a considerable strain on his family, as well as on the minister himself. As years progressed the tutor often recruited the assistance of one or more of his best pupils. Some of these went on to establish their own academies, but usually elsewhere. When a tutor died his academy disappeared, but succession was guaranteed by the fervour generated in able students who felt called to carry on the good work.

The first two academies were launched in 1663, the year after the great ejection; one at Coventry and another at Sheriffhales,[10] (near Shifnal) in Shropshire. This latter was in a very splendid manor house which is still standing, unlike the much more humble abodes which were usual in these early years. In spite of persecution these both lasted until the end of the 17th century.

Up until the Toleration Act of 1689, at the beginning of William and Mary's reign, just over twenty of these small academies had appeared, scattered across the land from Suffolk to the West Country and Wales; from London to West Yorkshire and the Lake District. But by the end of the century almost half of these were already extinct.[11] As these academies were designed to educate for the ministry they taught Latin, Greek and Hebrew, with Biblical Studies and Theology. Natural Philosophy (Science), Mathematics and Modern Languages were sometimes included. Tuition was normally in Latin, as was customary in the universities.[12]

A minute of the Presbyterian Fund,in 1725,[13] which at that time was concentrating support on the academies at Taunton, Findern and Carmarthen, gives us an insight into the sort of course they expected for theological students,

> 'None of the managers of this fund will encourage (the exhibitioners) being employed anywhere as ministers . . . unless it appears upon examination that they can render into English any paragraph of Tully's offices . . . that they read a psalm in Hebrew, translate into Latin any part of the Greek Testament to which they shall be directed, give a satisfactory account of their knowledge in the several sciences they studied at the Academy, and draw up a thesis upon any question that shall be proposed to them in Latin, and compose a sermon on a practical subject calculated for the improvement of a serious and well-disposed congregation.'

The first Academy in the North of England was at **Rathmell,**[14] near Settle in Ribblesdale. **Richard Frankland, M.A.**(Cantab.), himself a native of Rathmell, was ejected from his living at Bishop Auckland in County Durham in 1662, and returned to set up a

Rathmell in Ribblesdale – College Fold – remaining buildings from Richard Frankland's Academy.

ministry in and around his native village. He was an outstanding scholar, and when Cromwell was planning a new University at Durham, Frankland was among the people earmarked for this project.[15] But with the political changes his academic career took a very different turn, and Durham had to wait more than a century and a half before it had a university.

Many of the early tutors suffered harassment but none more so than Frankland, who moved location six times in all, finally ending up back at Rathmell.[16] Yet his itinerant Academy lasted for nearly thirty years, and accommodated over 300 pupils in that time. In the later years at Rathmell he had as many as eighty boarding in the little village at one time. John Cockin, the preacher from Holmfirth, visiting the village in 1812, reports the survival of

> 'traditions . . . respecting the "old college"'. It was an extensive establishment, bounded by a high wall, which enclosed an acre of ground. Over the gate of the yard was a large bell, which rang at stated times to summon the students to prayers and meals. Some of the buildings have been taken down, and those which are still standing are converted into cottage houses. There was a long row of windows to the different studies, most of which are now walled up . . . The garden and orchard were extensive, but are now converted into pasture land.[17]

This was obviously the Academy in its final phase during those later years.

The first move had come in 1674 when Frankland was invited to be minister at Natland near Kendal. Had not that move taken place he might have remained undisturbed and ignored at Rathmell, just as other early academies managed to weather these stressful years. But when persecution was stepped up and the Five Mile Act was applied with great rigour, being near the town of Kendal he was forced to leave Natland in 1683. Then within the next three years he was forced to move again three times, the last of these moves being to Attercliffe Hall in Sheffield. There he remained until the Toleration Act of 1689, when he decided to move back to Rathmell, where he was until his death in 1698. Frankland was Calvinist and said not to be very liberal; his style was described as high Presbyterian. Nevertheless the students who came to him included Episcopalians and Independents as well. Commentators refer to his 'broad platform', which apparently refers to his liberal attitude towards students admitted rather than to his Theology.

His only published work[18] came in the year before his death. It is a stout defence of the doctrine of the blessed Trinity. Nicholson and Axon[19] devote a chapter to it in their book, and whereas they are obviously not in sympathy with his doctrinal position they are unbiased and gracious in their presentation.

It was to the Academy at Rathmell that Robert Yates of Warrington sent his son Samuel to be educated to succeed him. The record states, 'Robert Yates devoted his "dear Samuel" and Mr. Jollie of Atherton his "young Timothy" upon the same day and together they were placed under the care of Mr. Frankland.'[20] This was in 1673; and in the following year Samuel, with his tutor and fellow students, moved to Natland. After the Academy he went to Edinburgh University where he gained his M.A. in 1677. He returned to Warrington to assist his father who was ill, and who died the following year. The son succeeded in the ministry, but only until 1683 when he himself died at the early age of 27.

This was about twenty years on from the time of the great ejection, and the next minister to succeed Samuel Yates was himself an ejected minister, from Formby. He was Peter Aspinwall,[21] an Oxford graduate, who before coming to Warrington was minister at Ashton-in-Makerfield. He was a man of independent means and was said to have preached freely – i.e. without payment. He was an elderly man when he died in 1696.

Sankey Street Academy - Warrington's first.

Aspinwall's successor was a most important figure in the history of Warrington non-conformity as he built the first chapel, and had an academy[22] in his home for nigh on half a century. **Charles Owen**[23] was born near Carmarthen. His parents were devout Anglicans. Yet all their nine children became zealous non-conformists. Three sons became ministers, the other two in Wales; and one of these, James, had an academy, first at Oswestry and later at Shrewsbury. Charles was educated at one of the London academies, that of John Ker at Bethnal Green.

Charles Owen came to Warrington at a time when persecution was subsiding. Many chapels were established in barns in those days, and his was no exception. Randle Myddleton was a blacksmith, whose forge jutted out into Sankey Street, with a small-holding behind. On this was his dwelling house, a brew house and a barn, as well as a small plot of land which he farmed. Charles Owen acquired the barn for use as his chapel, and took a lease, at 2/- per annum, from the Earl of Warrington. Sixteen years later he purchased all the land occupied by Middleton. The blacksmith's house became his home, and the smithy, which obtruded into Sankey Street, was sold to the town of Warrington to be pulled down (an early instance of street improvement).

On the land which he acquired at the rear of Sankey Street, was built, in the early years of the 18th century, the first Presbyterian

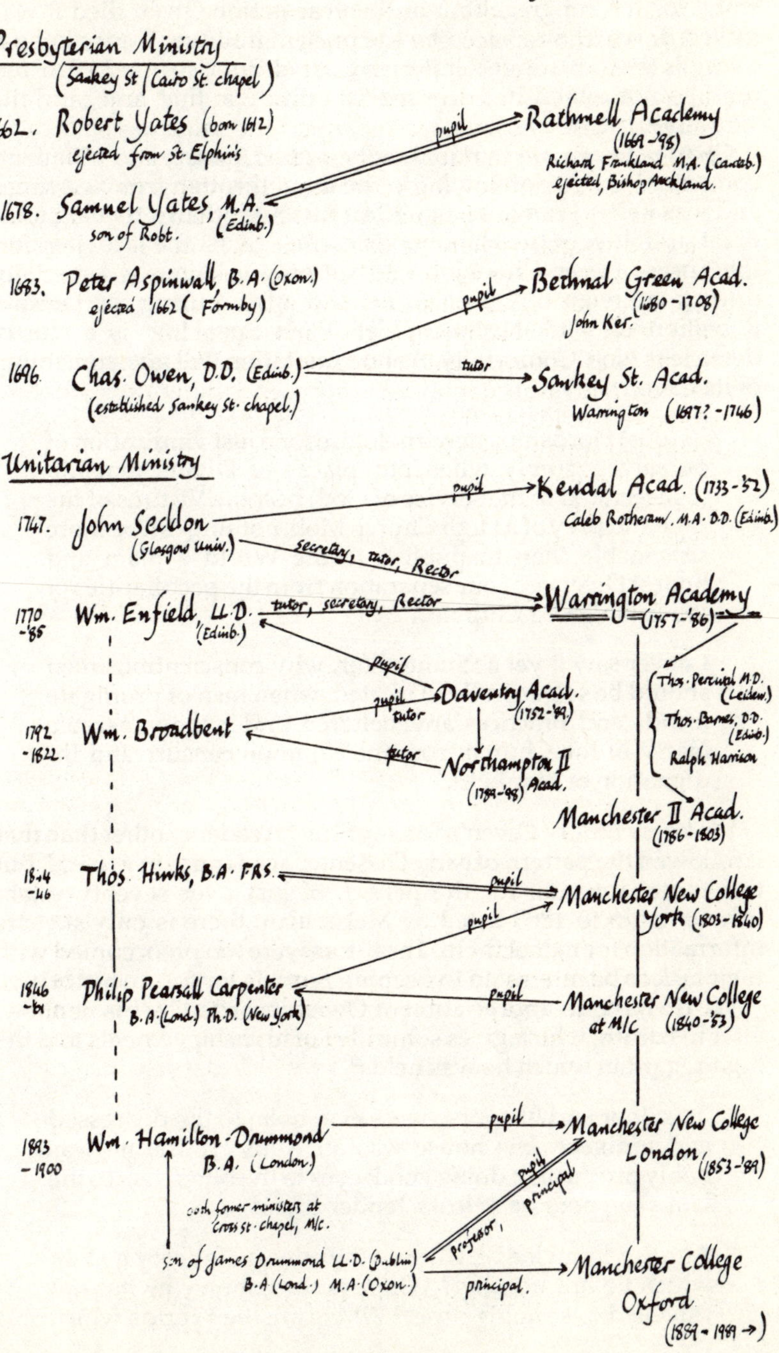
Warrington Dissent & the Nonconformist Academies.
Presbyterian Ministry
(Sankey St / Cairo St. chapel)
1662. Robert Yates (born 1612)
ejected from St. Elphin's
pupil
Rathmell Academy
(1669-98)
Richard Frankland M.A. (Cantab.)
ejected, Bishop Auckland.
1678. Samuel Yates, M.A. (Edinb.)
son of Robt.
1683. Peter Aspinwall, B.A. (Oxon.)
ejected 1662 (Formby)
pupil
Bethnal Green Acad.
(1680-1708)
John Ker.
1696 Chas. Owen, D.D. (Edinb.)
(established Sankey St. chapel.)
tutor
Sankey St. Acad.
Warrington (1697? -1746)
Unitarian Ministry
pupil
Kendal Acad. (1733-'52)
Caleb Rotheram, M.A. D.D. (Edinb.)
1747. John Seddon
(Glasgow Univ.)
secretary, tutor, Rector
1770 -'85 Wm. Enfield, LL.D. (Edinb.)
tutor, secretary, Rector
Warrington Academy
(1757-'86)
Thos. Percival M.D. (Leiden)
Thos. Barnes, D.D. (Edinb.)
Ralph Harrison
pupil
Daventry Acad.
(1752-'89)
pupil
tutor
1792 -1822. Wm. Broadbent
tutor
Northampton II Acad.
(1789-'98)
Manchester II Acad.
(1786-1803)
1844 -46 Thos. Hinks, B.A. FRS.
pupil
Manchester New College
York (1803-1840)
pupil
1846 -61 Philip Pearsall Carpenter
B.A. (Lond.) Ph.D. (New York)
pupil
Manchester New College
at M/C (1840-'53)
1893 -1900 Wm. Hamilton-Drummond
B.A. (London)
pupil
Manchester New College
London (1853-'89)
both former ministers at
Cross St. chapel, M/c.
son of James Drummond LL.D. (Dublin)
B.A. (Lond.) M.A. (Oxon.)
pupil
principal
professor,
principal.
Manchester College
Oxford
(1889-1989 →)

Chapel, which stood for about 40 years, by which time it was too small for the congregation. In the year before Owen died it was pulled down and replaced by the present building, better known today as the Cairo Street Unitarian Chapel. But Cairo and Warrington had not established any special affinity at that time, and the side street did not yet exist.

Charles Owen was undoubtedly a good pastor and a patient, competent teacher of youth. But he lived through troubled times and was better known as a political dissenter than a theologian, a great upholder of the Hanoverian cause against the Jacobites and the Tories. He and his kind had suffered grievously, especially during the reign of Queen Anne, and again during the Jacobite Rebellion of 1715. His pamphlet 'Plain Speaking' is a sturdy defence of Non-Conformity. A short quotation will give something of its flavour,[24]

> 'If (our) Hardships may apologise for a just vindication of ourselves, surely when our places of Divine worship (consecrated to the service of God) become Victims of the rage and prey of a High Church Mob, nothing can be more seasonable than to publish to the World a plain and honest Defence of our separation from the peculiarities of the Established Church . . .
>
> I never saw it yet accounted for, why conscientious men should be so generally ill treated, when men of profligate Minds and Practices are sheltered under the venerable Name of the Church from the common censure and Indignation of Mankind.'

We know little of Owen's Sankey Street Academy other than that it followed the pattern of early Dissenter academies in general. But this is not unusual for the period; of just over seventy establishments up to 1800 listed by McLachlan, there is only sketchy information for half of them. The tutors were too preoccupied with their task to be interested in keeping records for future historians.

We do have an appreciation of Owen recorded by his nephew, after his death, which gives some idea of his achievements and the high regard in which he was held.[25]

> 'His door and his purse were ever open to the distressed and indigent. His house was an Alms House; he was nobly prodigal in doing good; eyes to the blind; feet to the lame; the poor have lost a tender friend . . .
>
> As to his knowledge, where is the mine of Philosophy into which he has not dug? Where is the country he has not travelled over in his closet? Where are the Worlds which

> he has not explored? And in what regions shall we find a language to which he was a stranger?
>
> Thus adorned and thus qualified, Heaven continued him to a good old age, yet even in the later periods of life he was old in nothing but in years and goodness.'

We know that the work of the Academy was interrupted in 1714 with the passing of the Schism Act, which declared that no person should teach the young, either in school or college or privately, without conforming to the Church of England and obtaining a Bishop's licence. This was a great blow to Dissenters, and threatened all the existing academies. Everything they had striven so hard to build up over half a century could suddenly be wiped out. But heaven smiled upon these stricken ministers. In the same year Queen Anne died and the Act was not enforced. With the advent of the Hanoverian Dynasty things became easier for the Dissenters, and although full religious liberty was still a long way off persecution was fading. After a short intermission the Sankey Street Academy resumed again and continued until Charles Owen died in 1746.

A few oblique references cast some light into the gloom and one of these is worthy of note for its style, if for no other reason. It refers to some correspondence of Jonathan Woodworth,[26]

> 'The author of these letters was a sober, godly, hopeful youth, a good scholler and one yt apply'd himself but too close to his studys. He devoted himself to ye ministry, and was sometimes under ye direction and Tutorage of ye Rev. Mr. Charles Owen of Warrington, till ye Scism Bill took place, and then Mr. Owen desisted and this young man went to Glasgow . . .'

A further fact which marked Owen's stature as a worthy tutor was the conferring of a Doctorate of Divinity upon him by the University of Edinburgh in 1728.[27] The Scottish universities regarded English Dissenters with great sympathy and were always ready to mark outstanding academic achievement with honorary degrees. Owen had already been in Warrington for more than thirty years by then, so there had been ample opportunity to assess his capabilities. It is obvious that the distinction was not lightly conferred.

Owen was author of a remarkable work on the Natural History of Serpents(1742).[28] This 'consists of a mixture of well-authenticated scientific material with ancient and modern myths, displaying an amazing breadth of knowledge in the author.'

Something of his philosophy is revealed in the dedication, where he poses the question,

> 'What is it that makes the great character, but knowledge in all its diversity, a sollicitousness for the spread of arts and sciences, excelling in one's particular station of Life, and being divinely forward to all the high offices of humanity?'

Ashley Smith concludes,

> 'As a programme of university education, combined with the emphasis in the previously quoted passage on the integration of the scientific part of the curriculum with the core-subject of theology, this would be hard to improve.'

Before going on to consider Warrington's more famous Academy in the latter part of the 18th century, it is necessary to return to Rathmell to trace the course of its successors and the influence they were to have on this new establishment.

Continuity in academic establishments is a well recognised feature and one that we have no difficulty in recognising in normal circumstances. Many examples may be cited, such as Oxford and Cambridge colleges, Eton and Rugby, Cheltenham Ladies College and Roedean, Stonyhurst and Ampleforth, Chetham's Hospital and Manchester Grammar School. All of these have a common pattern:– established in premises in one location, where they remain generation after generation, with personnel overlapping through the generations, one teacher replacing another as each retires or dies. Among the students:– brother following brother, son following father, uncles and nephews, cousins and family friends. Then there are libraries built up over time, which house archives and other records. There are portraits of great patrons with the more famous teachers and graduates, photographs of great cricket XIs and other sporting teams, as well as gifts and other memorabilia. There is furniture, probably inscribed by the penknives of countless youths, and other equipment. There is tradition and a philosophy, academic aims and style. There is continuity in management, backed by trust funds, endowments and investments.

In the case of the Dissenter Academies however, the matter is not so clear cut, especially in the early generations. Circumstances were very much against the sort of smooth continuity which has just been described; of their nature they were *transient and itinerant*, and yet patterns of continuity can be marked out.

A few exceptions should be noted, the most remarkable being Bristol Baptist College,[29] which has already celebrated its tercentenary. It has changed premises, but at those times existing staff and students have moved directly into the new buildings, and these have all been within a short radius in the city. It is now an affiliated college of Bristol University. The Memorial College at Aberystwyth is another, which claims direct descent from Brynllwarch Academy in Carmarthen, founded by Samuel Jones, M.A.(Oxon.)[30] about 1672. Unlike the Bristol College it has operated in different locations.

The Academy founded by the redoubtable Selina, Dowager Countess of Huntingdon at Trefecca[31] in Breconshire in 1768, moved to Cheshunt, then to Cambridge to be affiliated with the University. From then onwards it had a close association with the Presbyterian Westminster College, and in recent times the two have been amalgamated under the Westminster label. Would Selina have approved? It is extremely doubtful.

Other academies had much more tenuous links, but nevertheless fall into broad groupings. The London academies were numerous and diverse, but one group, mainly Evangelical, which had links and continued, gradually coalesced to form New College in 1850, which was affiliated to London University until the College expired in 1977.

The Independents had groupings with their own specific ethos. This is clearly expressed by Wadsworth in his book on the Yorkshire United Independent College where he states,[32]

> 'In 1756 the Rev. James Scott began his work as tutor of the newly established academy at Heckmondwike in the West Riding of Yorkshire. The academy was founded by the Northern Education Society for training of orthodox and evangelical ministers to counteract the religious apathy and heresy, or as the Society expressed it, "*to dispel the clouds of Socinian darkness*" which then overspread the country. From that academy in a house in Spen Valley can be traced the unbroken stream which leads, *though with some meanderings and dry seasons,* to Emm Lane (Bradford) and the present Yorkshire Independent College.'

This Yorkshire college amalgamated in 1958 with the Lancashire Independent College, which traced its descent back to Roby's Academy founded in 1803.[33] There was a further merger in 1968 with The Western College, Bristol, which had roots in the West Country – Ottery St. Mary (1752), Bridport (1765), Taunton (1780), Exeter (1829) and Plymouth (1845) – and The Paton Congregational College, Nottingham. In 1984 there was a further sharing of facilities to form 'The Northern Federation for Training in Ministry', incorporating the Baptists and the Unitarians, which is affiliated to Manchester University.

It is interesting that Wadsworth should trace 'an unbroken stream which leads, *though with some meanderings and dry seasons*' to a further stage in development, because this is precisely the problem we confront in tracing the descent from Rathmell to Warrington and Manchester.

Alexander Gordon, M.A., the distinguished nineteenth century non-conformist historian, and a graduate of Manchester New College at London, expressed a similar view to Wadsworth when he grouped the academies of Rathmell, Manchester I, Whitehaven/Bolton, and Kendal together with Warrington and Manchester II as **'The Northern Academy'**. He said, 'The lineal succession is perfect. It is not only one Academy after another, but is Academy out of Academy'. However, turning to Rathmell's other successor – Attercliffe – he states, 'It is not in our list and we do not want it there,' – an expression so vehement that it suggests a degree of prejudice.

Irene Parker in 1914[34] rejected this thesis of Gordon's. She wrote,

> 'Even if it be allowable (and it is not) to group together Rathmell, Chorlton's (Manchester), Whitehaven, Bolton and Kendal as the Northern Academy, it is not possible to regard Warrington, *which was an entirely new foundation*, as descended from these earlier academies'.

V.D.Davis in his History of Manchester College (1932)[35] accepts and develops Gordon's thesis; **McLachlan** (1943)[36] in a detailed and closely reasoned section of his 'History of the Warrington Academy' quotes both Gordon and Parker. Eventually he sides with the latter. So, is the case closed?

To answer this question we must go back to consider the basic concept of academic continuity in relation to these early academies. It is clear that we must not expect to find the fully developed pattern, which obtains for instance in the ancient Oxbridge colleges, or to take a non-conformist example, the Bristol Baptist College. If this is what we expect then there will be no succession from the academies of the first century following the Restoration, apart from Bristol itself and Carmarthen/Aberystwyth, with Trefecca/Cheshunt following behind.

But which is more important, the material manifestations of continuity, or the personal and spiritual? As fundamentalists and evangelicals will rightly stress, Christianity grew in a domestic setting without settled premises; there was no Vatican Palace, no St. Peter's, no Canterbury Cathedral, no Westminster Abbey, no Dissenter Chapels, no Quaker meeting houses, no Essex Hall. Do any of us therefore argue that there can have been no 'Apostolic Succession'. Many will assert strongly that Christianity would be more healthy if we were to return to that model. In fact that is precisely what many dissenters, particular Independents, have done and are still doing.

In this way it seems reasonable to argue that succession among the early academies can be deduced from the spiritual and personal, but not from material factors; perhaps the emphasis should be on progression rather than succession as the story unfolds.

When Frankland died one of his former pupils, **John Chorlton**, was already established as assistant to Henry Newcome at Manchester, where the Cross Street Chapel was founded. Chorlton was invited to return to Rathmell to carry on what was by then a thriving institution.[37] He chose instead to establish the first **Manchester Academy** and invited some of Frankland's remaining pupils to join him there. Apart from the fact that he did not wish to abandon his ministry in the city, his main reason was that students would have access to the excellent library at Chetham's Hospital (a school and not a medical foundation).

Had Chorlton returned to Rathmell, continuity would not be disputed, but would his teaching have been any different? He inherited something of Frankland's spirit, and a few of his students, but not his premises. Chorlton's academy lasted for fifteen years and was still in the time of active persecution. In 1703 he was prosecuted for keeping a public academy, but in spite of this interruption he was able to carry on.

Five years before the Manchester Academy finished, one of its pupils, **Thomas Dixon**,[38] who had moved to **Whitehaven** as Minister, set up an Academy there. This overlap is used as an argument against continuity, but again it is the tutor/pupil relationship and the spirit carried on which signify. Dixon's standing as an academic and a teacher was rewarded early by an M.A. conferred on him in 1709 by the University of Edinburgh. He was said to have been a competent theologian who then went on to study medicine. In 1718 he gained his M.D. degree from Aberdeen. In 1723 he moved to **Bolton**, where, in addition to his ministry and teaching, while continuing his Academy, he also engaged in medical practice. This is a remarkable combination; he must have been a man of extraordinary energy and stamina, but it is scarcely surprising that he died at the early age of 49, said to be from overstrain.

The combination is not unique however. John Ker, of the Bethnal Green Academy,[39] had an M.D. from Leiden as well as his Edinburgh M.A., and Thomas Hill at Findern Academy[40] is referred to as minister and village doctor. Studies at Whitehaven and Bolton included Theology, Scripture, Classics, Mathematics and a modicum of basic Science. About forty years after leaving Bolton one of its pupils, John Taylor, D.D., became the first tutor and Principal at Warrington Academy.

Another pupil from Whitehaven, **Caleb Rotheram**, set up an Academy in **Kendal**[41] about ten years after Dixon had moved to Bolton, and five years after his death – another 'dry season'! It is said of Rotheram that, 'He was of a most communicative temper, and his lectures were rather the open information of a friend, than the dictates of a master. As an impartial lover of truth, he encouraged the most free and unbounded inquiry after it in every branch of science'. He is said to have excelled in Mathematics and Natural Philosophy (Science). He taught the other branches of Philosophy and Divinity with great success, and notes were taken in Shorthand. In Doctrine Rotheram was said to have been an Arian. Certainly many of his students went that way, but there is some doubt about his own position. Nicholson and Axon quote Hawkes' (1839) statement[42] that, 'The sentiments of Dr. Rotheram were certainly not orthodox, though not avowedly Unitarian. His views on the Trinity seem to have been far removed from the Church of England, and were probably the most moderate form of Sabellianism.' In a later chapter[43] they state that, 'Caleb Rotheram, junior, (1732-96) was the first of the Kendal ministers who became a Unitarian in the modern acceptation of the word.' They conclude, 'Whether Sabellian or Arian, all authorities allow that Rotheram (senior) loved and taught liberty of thought.'

Kendal Academy, like Whitehaven/Bolton before it, had support from the Presbyterian Fund. A few students also had support from the Baptist Fund and the Lady Hewley Fund. In just under twenty years Rotheram educated about 120 laymen and 56 divinity students.

Like Charles Owen at Warrington and Dixon at Whitehaven, Rotheram had degrees conferred on him by the University of Edinburgh during his career as a tutor. When the Academy was about ten years old he was awarded an M.A.. Later the same year (1743) he submitted a dissertation which gained him his D.D.

Two pupils from Kendal came later to Warrington. John Seddon[44] followed Charles Owen at the Sankey Street Chapel and played a major part in bringing the new Academy to Warrington in 1757. George Walker[45] came in time to that Academy as a tutor and later went to its successor at Manchester. Another John Seddon,[46] (second cousin of the Warrington minister),

Kendal Academy building in Market Place (as given in Nicholson & Axon, 1915). Unitarian chapel behind, through archway.

went to Cross Street Chapel, Manchester. John Wilkinson,[47] said to have been the greatest Iron Master of the eighteenth century, was another pupil. His daughter Mary later married Joseph Priestley, who taught her brothers at Nantwich and Warrington.

The scientific apparatus from Kendal passed to Warrington Academy and later to Hackney College.

When Frankland was at **Attercliffe**, one of his earlier pupils from Rathmell, **Timothy Jollie**, was an Independent Minister at Sheffield. This is the same Timothy Jollie who had gone up to Rathmell with Samuel Yates of Warrington. After Frankland returned to Rathmell, Jollie carried on an Academy, first in his own house, and then in Attercliffe Hall[48] where Frankland had operated. Jollie is reputed to have been distinguished for his benevolent manner and gift of oratory, rather than for his scholarship. It is said that the curriculum was narrow; that little attention was given to Classics and Hebrew. Joseph Mottershead, later minister at Cross Street Chapel, Manchester, records that 'Jollie *forbade Mathematics as tending to scepticism and infidelity*, though many by stealth made considerable progress in that way'. Archbishop Thomas Secker, another old pupil, reported that 'only the old philosophy of the schools was taught and that neither ably or diligently'. Also that he was 'utterly unacquainted with logic'. Jollie's main objective seems to have been 'to train effective preachers who were sound in the faith', the predominant aim among the Independents. Yet in spite of all these strictures McLachan remarks that 'few academies can boast a roll of students so distinguished as Attercliffe'. They included John Bowes, who became Lord Chancellor of Ireland; Nicholas Saunderson, a blind student who became Professor of Mathematics at Cambridge; John Jennings of Kibworth; and Dr. Benjamin Grosvenor, a distinguished scholar, who in time bequeathed his library to Warrington Academy.

Gordon[49] obviously saw Jollie's Academy as something of an aberration, because of its style, which differed considerably from that of Frankland's; but perhaps also because Jollie was Independent rather than Presbyterian. Only in such ways can Gordon's rejection be understood. Another commentator is more subtle, referring to John Jennings, who was educated at Attercliffe, as 'Frankland's pupil's pupil';[50] thus acknowledging the succession whilst apparently demeaning the link.

Allowing for Gordon's attitude to Jollie and his Academy, it is much more difficult to understand his failure, and that of others since his time, to acknowledge the connection between the Academies of the Kibworth, Northampton, Daventry axis and Warrington Academy. The indebtedness of Warrington to Bolton and Kendal, was no greater than that to the Midlands group, which provided four outstanding tutors over the years, including John Aikin who was at Warrington longer than any other individual, and who, with his family, had such a remarkably cohesive influence on both the academic and social life of the Academy there.

If Miss Parker's rejection of Gordon's Northern group is somewhat pedantic, then Gordon's own failure to acknowledge the Midland's link would seem to be myopic. The second Academy at Warrington (1757-86) was indeed quite a new venture, on an entirely new plan. But without the experience and learning gained from these earlier groups this later development could not have occurred in the way that it did.

A problem has also been posed by the fact that New College, London,[51] claims descent from Rathmell, through the Midlands' group. This succession, which McLachlan applauds,[52] is neither more nor less justified than what is here claimed for Warrington. Nor need either claim be seen as exclusive. It is difficult to understand, when McLachlan is prepared to accept a line of succession from Rathmell, through Attercliffe, Kibworth, Northampton, Daventry, and Wymondley, to New College, London, how he can reject Gordon's line from Rathmell through Whitehaven, Bolton and Kendal to Warrington and Manchester. The complex chart at the beginning of Ashley-Smith's book[53] shows just what an intricate web of interconnections existed between so many of the academies and colleges, so that multiple relationships are common.

John Jennings, B.A.(Oxon.) was Rector at Hartley Wespall in Hampshire. Ejected in 1662, he became Chaplain to Mrs. Pheasant at Langton Hall in Leicestershire; and then with the Toleration Act in 1689 he moved to the nearby village of Kibworth Harcourt, where he established a Dissenting Chapel. Two of his sons feature in the history of the academies. The eldest, **John**, was educated at Attercliffe, as mentioned above; he returned to succeed his father as Minister at Kibworth in 1701. Then in 1715 he established his Academy there.[54] David went to London, where he was educated at Moorfields Academy and went on to become a tutor at Hoxton Academy (another predecessor of New College). He was one of the few who had his degree from the University of St. Andrews.

It is of interest to note that the younger John married Anna Laetitia, daughter of Sir Francis Wingate, the Justice who committed John Bunyan to Bedford Gaol,[55] and who therefore merits some back-handed credit for 'Pilgrim's Progress'. A grand daughter, Ann, married the Rev. James Belsham, a dissenter. Bunyan would have felt himself well avenged had he known that two children of his persecutor had married non conformist clergymen. Wingate's grandchildren included the Rev. Thomas Belsham and

Jane Jennings, who married John Aikin, D.D., two more of the same to add to Bunyan's bag.

The point has already been made that family ties contribute to the pattern of academic continuity. The **family group of Jennings, Aikin and Belsham** bears this out in their close ties with the Academies of Kibworth, Northampton Daventry and Warrington. Philip Doddridge, not a blood relation, although he might have been had he been accepted by his first love – Jennings' daughter[56] (the same Jane who later married John Aikin) – was closely connected with these families. He was educated by Jennings at Kibworth. John Aikin was his pupil at Northampton Academy, and later, when Aikin had a school at Kibworth, Doddridge's son was one of his pupils. In later generations, Charles Wellbeloved, Principal at Manchester College, York, and John Kenrick, who became his son-in-law and assistant, joined the same family tree.

Kibworth Academy was small and shortlived, but had it not been for the untimely death of Jennings in 1723 at only thirty-five years, it might well have been one of the greatest. Philip Doddridge, its most distinguished pupil, has left us a detailed account of the course of studies, which was remarkably wide; including the Classics and Hebrew, Scripture, Logic, Ethics, Theology, Mathematics, Science, History, Geography, English Literature and French. In this latter he reports,[57] 'We . . . read the phrases and dialogues from French into English *without regarding the pronunci-*

Kibworth Harcourt, Leicestershire (A6 road) – Old White House (formerly plastered and whitewashed) site of John Jennings Academy.

Chapel and manse, where Jennings, Doddridge and Aikin ministered (Independent/ Congregational)

ation, with which Mr. Jennings was not acquainted'. Conversation in Latin was obligatory for part of the time; drama readings were an important contribution to language development. In Theology Doddridge stresses that Jennings always encouraged the greatest freedom of inquiry, a feature which keeps cropping up in the group of academies here being considered. Students were obliged to undertake preaching at the end of their course, either in Kibworth Chapel or further afield, to give them experience and confidence. Doddridge also mentions the free access they had to the tutor's library; some of the contents of which passed into his own library at Northampton, which was transferred in time to Wymondley, then to Coward College and eventually to New College, London. When this last expired in 1977 the books finally came to rest in Dr. Williams's Library in Gordon Square.[58]

Following Jennings' death Doddridge moved to Market Harborough, where he transferred the Academy before moving on to **Northampton** in 1729, to establish what McLachlan describes as 'in many ways the most famous of nonconformist seminaries'.[59] Doddridge was, for a time, Jennings' successor in the ministry at Kibworth, but did not attempt to continue the Academy there. So there was again something of a 'dry season'.

Dissenting tutors were still not entirely free from interference, and early on Doddridge at Northampton was challenged by a neighbouring vicar who asserted his own sole right to impart religious instruction in the parish.[60] He was cited to appear before the diocesan chancellor, Dr. Reynolds, to compel him to take out an ecclesiastical licence, which would of course mean conforming. The matter was referred to Judges at Westminster Hall, but in the end King George II himself intervened to quash the case. During the course of these proceedings the Academy was attacked by a Jacobite mob, to which the authorities turned a blind eye. Persecution was still a popular pastime, even if it no longer had the effective backing of officialdom. But royal intervention was no novelty. Frankland, in his later years at Rathmell, had enjoyed the protection of William III, which saved his Academy.[61]

At first Doddridge was disposed to cater only for the training of Ministers, until David Jennings prevailed on him to widen the provision. He argued:[62] 'The support of our interest comes from the laity, and they will not be constrained to bring up all their sons either as ministers or dunces.' They should not be driven, 'to send their sons, who are designed for physicians, lawyers or gentlemen to Oxford or Cambridge, or to make them rakes in foreign universities'.

The course at Northampton was broad, not unlike that at Kibworth. But now there was a significant break with tradition, which previous academies had carried forward from the universities. Latin was dropped as the language of tuition and study, to be replaced by English, 'a welcome relief from a tiresome linguistic strain'.[63] Not all academies followed suit, but the fashion had changed, and many did from then on. Every student was obliged to master Rich's system of Shorthand, as adapted, improved and used by Doddridge himself.

References given during lectures were 'numerous, comprehensive and representative of both sides in every controversial question. Every appearance of bigotry or uncharitableness was checked, and students were bidden to take their Divinity not from any man or body of men, but from the Bible itself',[64] again echoing the attitude at Kibworth. Science was not a particularly strong feature, but was not neglected.

Village preaching was again encouraged for the Divinity students, and Northampton became a noted centre of missionary activity. Doddridge was the first to have an academy library. He

Northampton Academy – town house of the Earl of Halifax leased to Philip Doddridge – Sheep Street.

lectured to his students on the books available in it, so that they might be encouraged to read widely. He made a charge of one guinea for the use of the library, to get a fund for the purchase of books, and a similar charge was made for the use of scientific apparatus.

This Academy had support from The Congregational Fund Board, The Presbyterian Fund, The Coward Trust, and from the Countess of Huntingdon. In return Independents, Presbyterians, Baptists and Calvinistic Methodists got ministers educated at Northampton. Of some two hundred students, one hundred and twenty went into the ministry.

Like others before him Doddridge was recognised by Scotland, as Aberdeen[65] conferred on him a D.D. eight years after he started teaching. In time he became much sought after as a consultant.[66] As well as by his own, he was consulted by eminent Anglican divines, by John Wesley, and by influential lay men. The subjects included literary, ecclesiastical, doctrinal and academic matters. We find him noting in his diary[67] that he has written between fifty and sixty letters in the past fortnight 'having no secretary'.

He was a devout man, and today he is mainly remembered for the hymns he wrote, which are valued for their deep spirituality as well as for their literary merit.

Among many distinguished students at Northampton were John Aikin and Stephen Addington, both of whom later succeeded in the ministry at Kibworth. Also Caleb Ashworth who moved the Academy to Daventry after Doddridge's death, with Samuel Clarke and Thomas Robins who became tutors at Daventry. Later on John Aikin and Nicholas Clayton moved to Warrington Academy as tutors.

At this point there occurs a digression in this tale of academies. John Aikin became minister at Kibworth in 1749. But soon afterwards his health deteriorated; spitting of blood and shortness of breath are mentioned, and an accident in which he was thrown from a horse may have been a contributory cause. But it is also possible that he may have contracted tuberculosis, as he himself believed, and he was certainly asthmatic. In any case it put paid to his career as a preacher and he was obliged to seek other employment. Stephen Addington succeeded him as minister in 1752, but Aikin remained in Kibworth for the next six years. During that time he had a primary school for boys and one young lady, his daughter Anna Laetitia. Other pupils included their cousin Thomas Belsham, and Doddridge's son.[68]

In this occupation Aikin continued until appointed to Warrington in 1758. Stephen Addington then took over the school, together with the ministry. He may have continued it for as long as twenty years. In 1784 he moved to Hoxton Academy at Mile End as tutor.

The new Academy at **Daventry**[69] (1752-1789) was called '**Doddridge Academy**', in honour of him whose demise had brought about the change. He had nominated as his successor **Caleb Ashworth**, who did as had been done so often in the past and moved the Academy to where he was Minister.

Daventry overlapped with Warrington, starting five years earlier and remaining open six years later. It did not have the same degree of planning or the launch that Warrington had. It did not have the purpose-built premises but remained in the original, leased building. It did not have as many students; the total was 274, whereas Warrington, in eleven years less, topped 400. And yet, in the ways it developed there were many similarities. It had a succession of tutors, and always several at the one time who specialised in particular subjects or groups of subjects. It attracted a succession of very able men.

Thomas Belsham, who was one of its students, then tutor and eventually its final Principal, seemed to believe that it might be over-reaching itself when he said to a group of students, 'If there is any fault in the course of study here, it is that there is too great a variety of objects proposed to your attention.'[70]

Daventry Academy, Sheaf Street. URC chapel behind, through the arcl (formerly Independent)

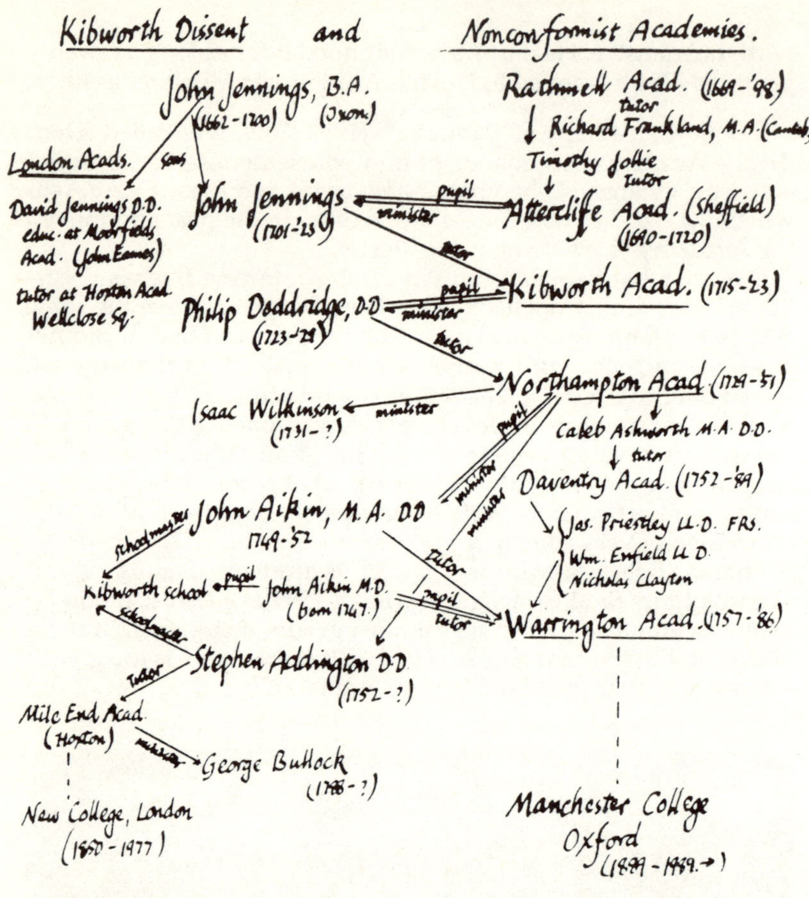

Notes

John Jennings (1633-1700) ejected 1662. Hartley Wespall, Hants. then tutor to Mr. Noyes at Tickwell, subsequently chaplain to Mr. Pheasant at Langton Hall (Leics.) 1689 – Toleration Act, moved to Kibworth Harcourt.

John Jennings (1687-1723) married Anna Laetitia, dau of Sir Francis Wingate & Lady Anne Annesley; 2 Wingate daus married Non-Conformist clergymen (Bunyan's revenge!)

John Aikin D.D. (1713-'80) married Jane Jennings, dau of John Jennings (jr)

John Aikin M.D. (1747-1822) m. Martha Jennings, grand-dau of John Jennings (jr), his mother's niece

Anna Laetitia Aikin (1743-1825) Mrs. Barbauld. dau. of John Aikin D.D. educ. at Kibworth school (w. the boys), & informally at Warrington Academy.

Academic Dissenters —— Kibworth family with connections.

Arthur Annesley – first Earl of Anglesey (Lord Privy Seal to Charles I)

Sir Francis Wingate = Lady Anne Annesley

Rev. John Jennings B.A. (Oxon.) (1633–1700) = Mary Green

John Aikin (1664–1756) = Anne Bentall

Thos. Wooward = Frances Wingate; John W.; Anna Laetitia Wingate = Rev. John Jennings (1687–1723); Rev. David Jennings D.D. (St. Andrews) (1691–1762)

Rev. James Belsham = Ann Woodward; Arthur Jennings = Martha Cornwall; John J.; Francis J.; Jane Jennings (1714–'85) = Rev. John Aikin, M.A. D.D. (Aberdeen) (1713–'80)

Betsy Belsham (1743–1819) m. Rev. Timothy Kenrick of Exeter (1758–1804); Rev. Thos. Belsham (1750–1829); John Kinder = Anna Laetitia Jennings; Martha Jennings = John Aikin, M.D. (Leiden) (1747–1822); Anna Laetitia Aikin (1743–1825) = Rev. Rochemont Barbauld (1749–1808)

Rev. Chas. Wellbeloved (1769–1858) = Anne Kinder; Arthur A. (1773–1834); Geo. Aikin (1774–1847); Chas. Rochemont Aikin (1775–1846); Anne Wakefield dau of Rev. Gilbert Wakefield, B.A.; Edmond Aikin 1780–1820; Lucy Aikin (1781–1846) family archivist & recorder

Chas. Wellbeloved; Laetitia Wellbeloved = Rev John Kenrick M.A. (Glasgow) (1788–1877)

Notes

1) Sir Francis Wingate was the justice who committed John Bunyan to Bedford gaol for unlicenced preaching; his daughter & a grand-dau. married dissenting ministers (Bunyan's posthumous revenge!)

2) Rev. Philip Doddridge, D.D. (1702–'51) was not related, but had many connections with these families; he was educated at Kibworth Acad. by John Jennings & John Aikin DD. was his pupil at Northampton Academy.

3) John Aikin's pupils at his Kibworth School in the 1750s included Doddridges son, his own son & daughter, & their cousin Thos. Belsham.

4) The Barbaulds had no children of their own, but adopted & reared Mrs. Barbauld's nephew – Charles Rochemont Aikin.

5) Rev. Charles Wellbeloved was principal of Manchester College at York, where John Kenrick became his assistant.

6) John Kenrick was eldest son of Rev. Timothy Kenrick of Exeter, by his first marriage; T.K. had been a tutor at Daventry & later established the third Exeter Academy, where John became a pupil; T.K. married Eliz. Belsham in 1794, & died in 1804.

The attitude to Philosophy and Theology was liberal in the extreme. Priestley records[71] that it was, 'In a state peculiarly favourable to the serious pursuit of truth, as the students were about equally divided upon every question of much importance . . . The tutors also were of different opinions; Dr. Ashworth taking the orthodox side of every question, and Mr. Clark, the sub-tutor, that of heresy, though always with the greatest modesty.'

Robert Hall,[72] a famous Baptist divine, views heterodoxy in rather a different light, describing Daventry as, 'This vortex of unsanctified speculation and debate.' He says, 'The majority of such as are educated there became more distinguished for their learning than for the fervour of their piety, or the purity of their doctrine.'

Daventry, like Warrington, was drifting towards Unitarianism, and this came to a head when Thomas Belsham was Principal. In 1789, when his position was beyond doubt, he resigned and moved to Hackney College. The Coward Trust (Congregational) which was in control of the Academy then moved it back to Northampton. Many of the students had support from the Presbyterian Fund, so to the end it remained rather mixed in its allegiance. Like Warrington it would be quite wrong to refer to it as a Unitarian seminary.

The main interest which Daventry has in the present connection is that it educated two leading Warrington tutors. Joseph Priestley was that Academy's first new pupil,[73] a fact which is commemorated with a stone plaque on the face of the building which still stands in Sheaf Street. William Enfield is the other, who came to Warrington following the death of John Seddon, to take his place as minister at Sankey Street Chapel, tutor and Rector Academiae.

It will be seen now that the group of academies here reviewed provided Warrington with seven of its leading tutors; one from Bolton, and two each from Kendal, Northampton and Daventry. As a group they varied in many ways and this review has attempted to bring out their distinctive characteristics. But they also had a lot in common; diversity and a liberal approach being perhaps the common denominator, with emphasis on a broad education, broader than some of the other academies in their time, and broader also than the English Universities (Oxbridge), which were still very much in the doldrums.

There is no doubt that the academies at Kibworth, Northampton and Daventry were in the tradition of the Independents, and the ministries in the associated chapels remained Independent. Even today the chapel at Kibworth retains the Independent label, while Northampton and Daventry have moved to the United Reformed Church. But it is the academic tradition which we are considering here. Stress has already been drawn from various commentators and laid on the broad approach to contentious doctrinal issues in these academies. This contrasts with the much narrower 'orthodoxy' of the Lancashire and Yorkshire Independent Colleges, and of some of the London academies.

Lucy Aikin writing to Dr. Ellery Channing in America in the 1830s throws interesting light on denominational evolution amongst her family and their associates in the latter half of the 18th century, when she states:

> "Long before my time, my kindred – the Jennings's, the Belshams, my excellent grandfather Aikin, and his friend and tutor Doddridge – had begun to break forth out of the chains and darkness of Calvinism, and their manners softened with their system. My youth was spent among the disciples or fellow-labourers of Price and Priestley, the descendants of Dr. John Taylor, the Arian, or the society of that most amiable of men, Dr. Enfield. Amongst these there was no rigorism. Dancing, cards, the theatre, were all held lawful in moderation: in *manners*, the Free Dissenters, as they were called, came much nearer the church than to their own stricter brethren, yet in *doctrine* no sect departed so far from the Establishment."

We should not be seeking here a discreet group, leading only to Warrington Academy and Manchester, because the links between dissenter establishments as a whole are much too diffuse for that, but Warrington is a focus which draws together the group outlined. There are still those who will share the prejudices of Alexander Gordon aginst Attercliffe and its successors, but there is no gainsaying the vital influence of Aikin, Priestley, Clayton and Enfield, and consequently of the academies in which they were educated, on Warrington.

The charts which illustrate this thesis also underline another aspect of cohesion. This is the association between successive ministers in certain chapels and their education at related academies, or, even more important, their being tutors in these academies. Cross Street Chapel, Manchester,[74] is a particularly interesting example of this phenomenon.

It is worthy of note that in spite of the time which has elapsed, a surprising number of the buildings concerned still survive, right back to the little row of cottages in Rathmell, which bear Frankland's initials in stone over one of the rear windows. These Georgian forebears obviously built well, but this is another feature of a great educational heritage which succeeding generations have neglected.

In conclusion, two lines of descent have been traced from Rathmell, each with a rather different tradition. This does not belie their common heritage, in view of what has already been said as to Frankland's 'broad platform'. The northern group was Presbyterian drifting to Arianism; the Midlands tradition was Congregational (Independent), although in the academies of this group orthodoxy was not interpreted as rigidly as in the stricter Yorkshire and Lancashire Independent colleges. Eventually, when Daventry Academy is reached, the Arian drift manifests itself there also, until at crisis point that establishment is closed and the truck is hauled firmly back onto the main line with the return to Northampton.

There is little doubt that the narrower Congregational orthodoxy at its purest is, to a marked degree, opposed to speculation. A conflict is perceived between the aspirations of a broad and liberal education on the one hand, and a fundamentalist faith which seeks to be sheltered from liberal tendencies on the other.

Donald Davie[75] is severe in castigating Warrington Academy for its elite intellectualism, but the reverse of what he is criticising is narrow, illiberal, protectionist and equally exclusive. Admittedly the Arian drift carried some of its successors in the 19th century into an amorphous, rudderless, atheistic humanism.

But there were others who followed a different path: James Martineau, the spiritual leader of Manchester College when it was in London was monotheistic and Unitarian, but never agnostic; he did much to shield his students and followers from the sterility of scepticism.

His contemporary, John Henry Newman, in his book 'The Idea of a University'[76] favours a broad liberal education coupled with a well-informed faith. Augustine of Hippo in the 4th century, escaping from the esoteric intellectualism of the Manichees, did not abandon the fine classical education which made him one of the ablest scholars and writers in the early Christian church and which enlivened his born-again faith. The purist and fundamentalist can be ultimately as great a menace to faith as the arrogant intellectual.

Warrington Academy, which is about to be explored, owed a great deal to a mingling of traditions which it acquired from tutors who came from both sides of the Rathmell heritage, and it is time that this broad base should be acknowledged. There is no fundamental conflict between the educational philosophy of Jennings and Doddridge, with their successors who came to Warrington, on the one hand, and the Northern tutors on the other. Attercliffe may be rejected, as by Gordon, or accepted with reservation; in the final analysis this is an irrelevant distraction; it is the traditions, aspirations, system, educational philosophy and personnel transmitted from one stage to the next which really signify.

DODDRIDGE ACADEMY
JOSEPH PRIESTLEY L.L.D. F.R.S.
THEOLOGIAN and MAN of SCIENCE
STUDENT here
1752-1755.

Chapter 3
A PLANNED ACADEMY AND WHERE TO SITE IT

'I am very proud of my old town, and very jealous of its honour. I rejoice to see it first in everything . . . but most of all I wish to see it first in those high things which make for its eternal peace; which won it, once, its proudest name . . . I look to this (Lit. and Phil. Soc.) and similar societies to keep the torch alight and hand it on. It is well to be "the town of many industries". It was better to be "the Athens of England". And we may be that again.'

Alderman Bennett (1905)[1]

As the first century following the Restoration and Clarendon's legislation was drawing to a close, the Penal Laws were still on the statute book, but they were no longer applied with the original severity. Non-conformists, to whom many offices and occupations were still barred, had found new outlets for their talents, mainly in trade, commerce, and manufacturing. Many of their leading families were becoming quite prosperous.

The time had come to review the role and the operation of their academies.[2] These were no longer actively persecuted, and although they still suffered many disadvantages the time seemed ripe by the middle of the 18th century for growth and innovation. The capital had had a succession of varied academies but the new development was not to be there.

From early on the planners seem to have settled on the Mersey valley and the southern border of Lancashire, but choosing between the available options was to occupy several years, during which the nature of the scheme and its financing were also being explored and promoted.

Manchester, Warrington and Liverpool were obvious contenders and provided considerable support for the project. These towns, at that time, must not be confused with what they would become during the next century when the Industrial Revolution was established. All were much smaller and none had the status of a city.

Manchester was a powerful contender, with its strong traditions in education. It had its Collegiate church with the attached Chetham's Hospital (school) and its superb library,[3] which had been a particular attraction when the first Manchester Academy had been established in 1698. It also had its Grammar School. The non-conformist Cross Street Chapel, which was a venue for many of the discussions, had links with several of the older academies, and would be a focus again when the new establishment did move to Manchester later in the century.

Liverpool was less well-placed. It was a growing port, which had superseded Chester as the Dee became silted. Its non-conformists were quite an influential body, but an educational tradition had yet to be established. Also, in the era of stage coaches, it was some distance removed from the major roads, as there was no crossing of the Mersey below Warrington, except by ferry. As the debate developed, supporters of the project in Liverpool began to canvass for Ormskirk as the chosen site. However, this town had some of the same disadvantages – it lacked tradition and was still some distance from the main road north through Lancashire.

Warrington had advantages, but was not at once the obvious choice. It was well-placed geographically, and its non-conformist tradition was strong. Its first academy[4] had only recently come to an end after flourishing for almost half a century. The Presbyterian minister and tutor at the academy, was succeeded as minister by a keen young man, John Seddon, a recent graduate of Kendal Academy who was determined that the new project should come to

Sankey Street chapel, Warrington (now Cairo Street) site of Charles Owen's Academy.

Warrington. In the end his enthusiasm and tireless campaigning was rewarded, as will be related in the next chapter.

Warrington is an ancient town,[5] the establishment of which was inevitable from the first penetration by man into the area. The River Mersey meanders over the flat lands below Manchester, and then below Warrington it widens out into its estuary. Where the town was established was the lowest point at which the river could be forded, and that man had known this from early pre-historic times is borne out by the discovery of ancient trackways, together with settlements on the higher ground both north and south of the river. It was the natural gateway between Cheshire and Lancashire.

The Romans in their progress northwards used the ford and had a settlement at Wilderspool on the south bank of the river. Excavations in the past century have revealed that their town like its recent successor was an industrial settlement, and not one of their legionary fortresses.

During Saxon times a monk named Elphin,[6] thought to be of Welsh stock and probably from the nearby ecclesiastical school at Bangor-on-Dee, settled just north of the ford where the parish church bearing his name stands today, and where Warrington had its centre until after the Normans came. Was Elphin perhaps the first to bring an academic tradition to this place?

The Normans arrived not long after Hastings, and established their lordship alongside Elphin's settlement. The Boteler family[7] remained to dominate the town through five centuries and eighteen generations. About 1256 they made the ford redundant by bridging the river less than a mile downstream. Around the same time they brought in the Augustinian Friars and established them by Bridgefoot. This resulted in a shift of town centre from Church Street to Bridge Street.

The friars were preachers rather than teachers, but one of their number achieved academic fame in the 15th century. He was Thomas of Penketh who went on to Oxford where he established a reputation which took him to the University of Padua where he became Professor of Philosophy. His commentary on Duns Scotus is the oldest printed book in the town's library, pre-dating Caxton. But, as his academic career was away from Warrington he did not establish any tradition in the town.

The 16th Baron, Sir Thomas le Boteler, established one of the earliest Grammar Schools, in the reign of Henry VIII, and before his break with Rome. This survived until quite recently, when it merged with a nearby school to become comprehensive. It was Warrington's major academic achievement before the Academy.

The town, being an important bridgehead, was heavily involved in the Civil War, originally as a Royalist stronghold under the Earl of Derby, until he was defeated by a Parliamentary army under Sir

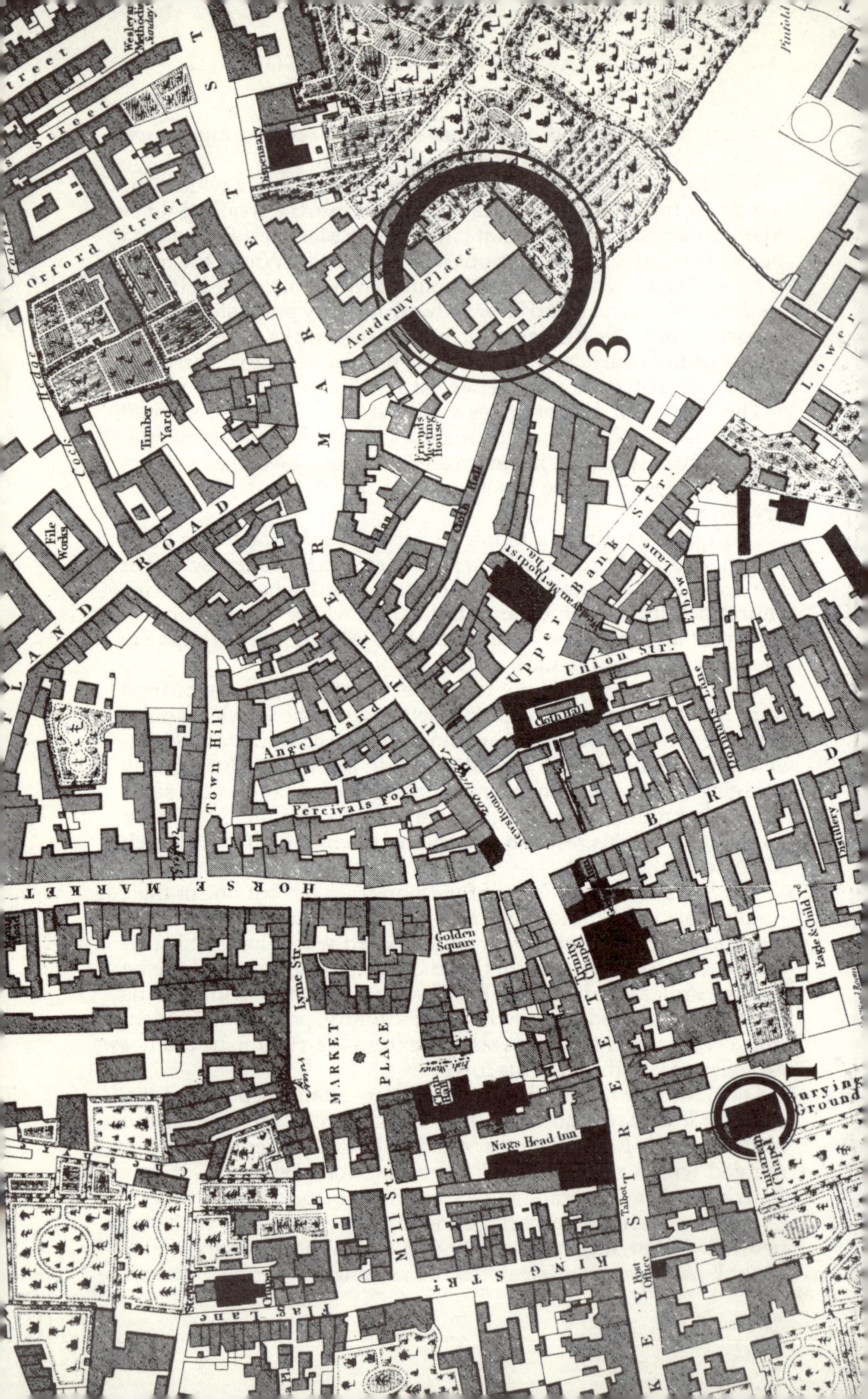

Orford Street
Academy Place
Timber Yard
Friends Meeting House
File Works
ROAD
Town Hill
Angel Yard
Percivals Fold
HORSE MARKET
Golden Square
Lyme Str.
MARKET PLACE
Nags Head Inn
Mill Str.
KING STR.
Flag Lane
Post Office
Talbot
Trinity Chapel
Unitarian Chapel
Burying Ground
Eagle & Child Yd.
Distillery
Union Str.
Cloth Hall
Upper Bank Str.
Lower
Elbow Lane
Pinfold
Dispensary
3
1

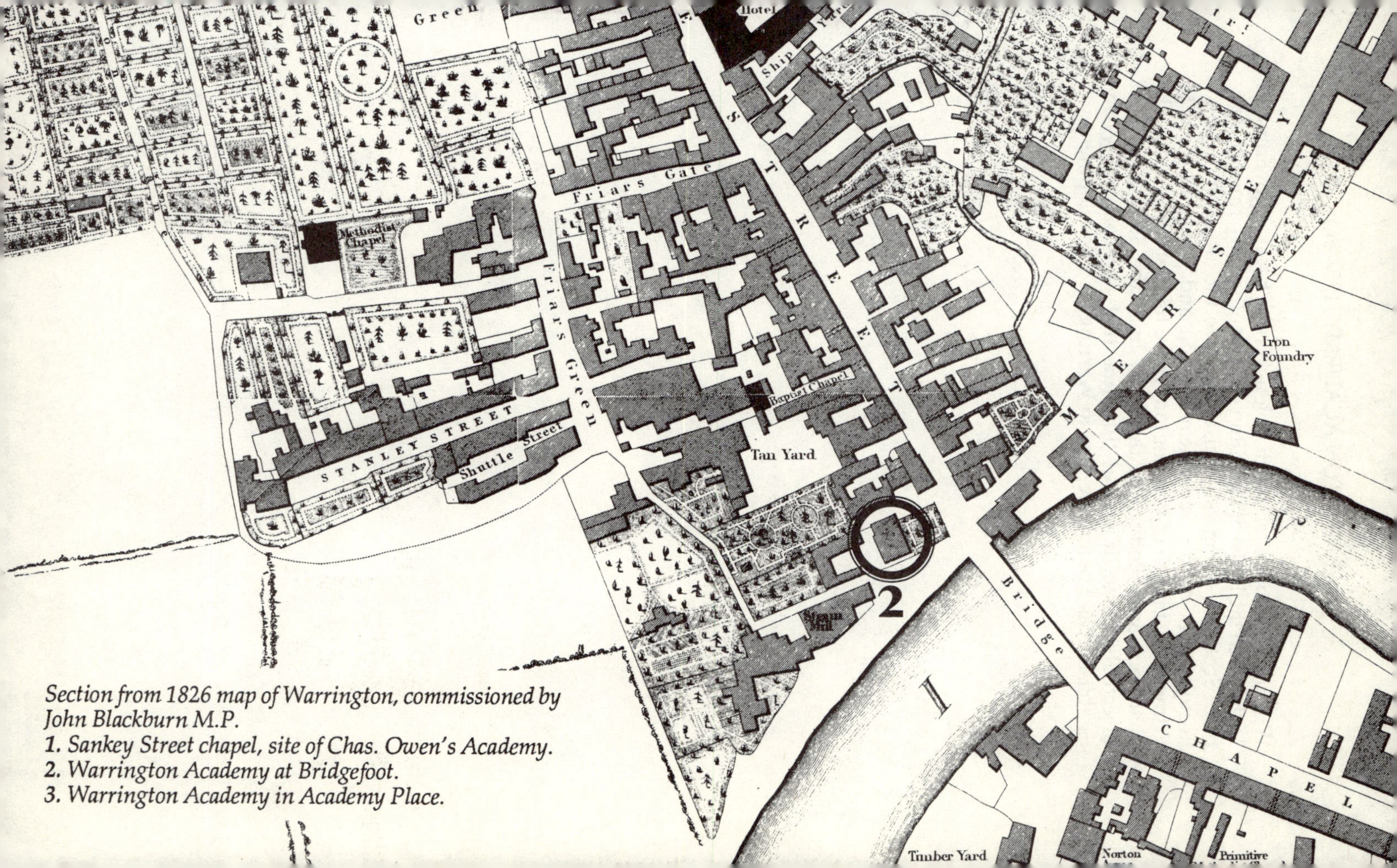

Section from 1826 map of Warrington, commissioned by John Blackburn M.P.
1. Sankey Street chapel, site of Chas. Owen's Academy.
2. Warrington Academy at Bridgefoot.
3. Warrington Academy in Academy Place.

William Brereton, after which Colonel Booth became governor. In 1648, when the Duke of Hamilton came south with a royalist army from Scotland, Cromwell himself came to the attack, inflicting a heavy defeat on the Scots near Preston and pursuing them to Winwick just north of Warrington where he beat them again. His victorious army lodged in the town until the Scots were sent dejectedly home. It was at this time that non-conformity was established as a potent element in Warrington's development.

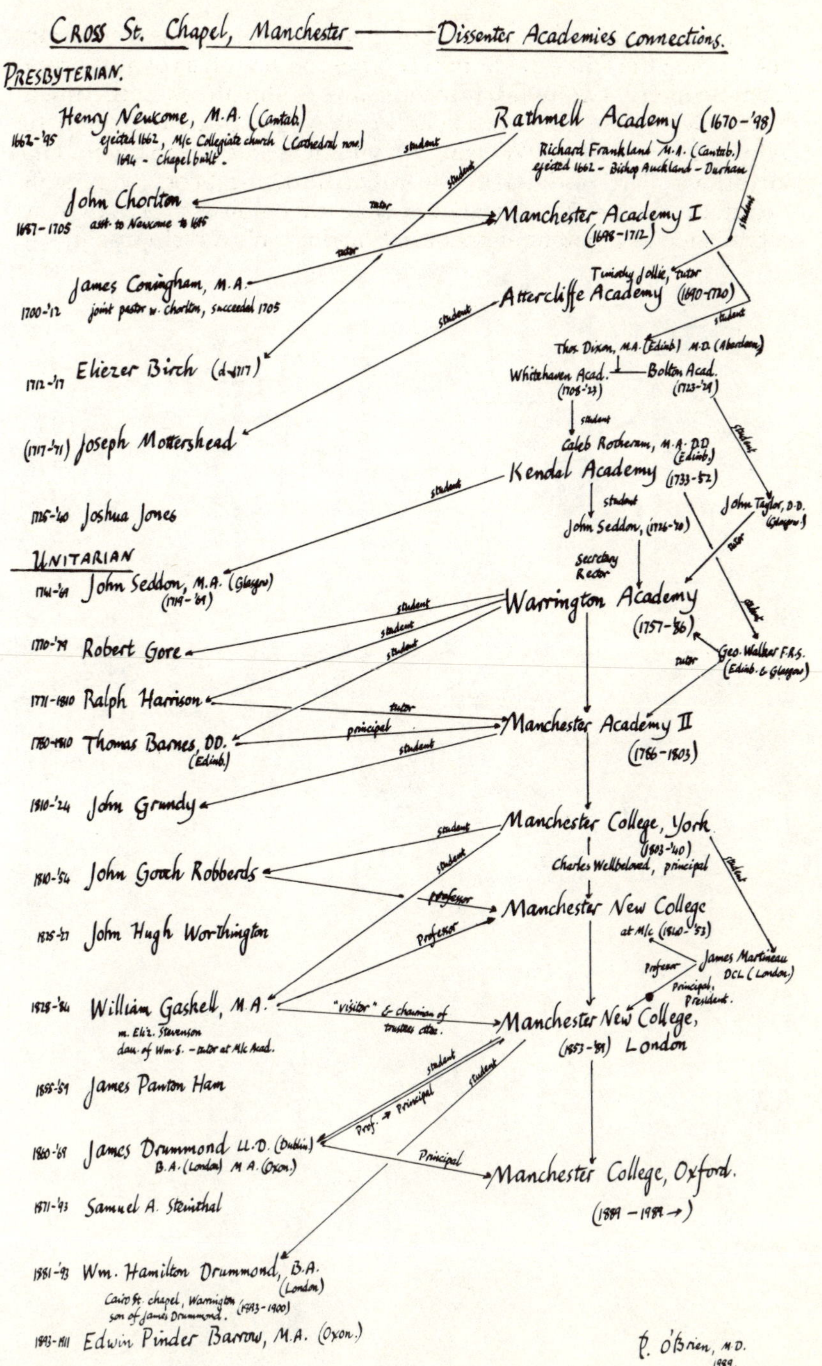
CROSS St. Chapel, Manchester — Dissenter Academies connections.
PRESBYTERIAN.
1662-'95 Henry Newcome, M.A. (Cantab.)
ejected 1662, M/c Collegiate church (Cathedral now)
1694 - Chapel built.
Rathmell Academy (1670-'98)
Richard Frankland M.A. (Cantab.)
ejected 1662 - Bishop Auckland - Durham
student
1687-1705 John Chorlton
asst. to Newcome to 1695
tutor
Manchester Academy I
(1698-1712)
1700-'12 James Coningham, M.A.
joint pastor w. Chorlton, succeeded 1705
Timothy Jollie, tutor
Attercliffe Academy (1690-1720)
1712-'17 Eliezer Birch (d.1717)
Thos. Dixon, M.A. (Edinb.) M.D. (Aberdeen)
Whitehaven Acad. (1708-'23)
Bolton Acad. (1723-'29)
(1717-'71) Joseph Mottershead
Caleb Rotheram, M.A. D.D (Edinb.)
Kendal Academy (1733-52)
1725-'60 Joshua Jones
John Seddon, (1726-'70)
John Taylor, D.D. (Glasgow)
UNITARIAN
1761-'69 John Seddon, M.A. (Glasgow) (1719-'69)
Secretary Rector
Warrington Academy (1757-'86)
1770-'79 Robert Gore
1771-1810 Ralph Harrison
Geo. Walker F.R.S. (Edinb. & Glasgow)
principal
1780-1810 Thomas Barnes, DD. (Edinb.)
Manchester Academy II (1786-1803)
1810-'24 John Grundy
Manchester College, York (1803-'40)
Charles Wellbeloved, principal
1810-'54 John Gooch Robberds
Professor
Manchester New College at M/c (1840-'53)
1825-'27 John Hugh Worthington
James Martineau DCL (London)
Principal, President.
1828-'84 William Gaskell, M.A.
m. Eliz. Stevenson
dau. of Wm S. - tutor at M/c Acad.
"visitor" & chairman of trustees etc.
Manchester New College, (1853-'89) London
1855-'59 James Panton Ham
Prof. → Principal
1860-'69 James Drummond LL.D. (Dublin) B.A. (London) M.A. (Oxon.)
Principal
Manchester College, Oxford. (1889 - 1989 →)
1871-'93 Samuel A. Steinthal
1881-'93 Wm. Hamilton Drummond, B.A. (London)
Cairo St. chapel, Warrington (1873-1900)
son of James Drummond.
1893-1911 Edwin Pinder Barrow, M.A. (Oxon.)
P. O'Brien, M.D. 1989.

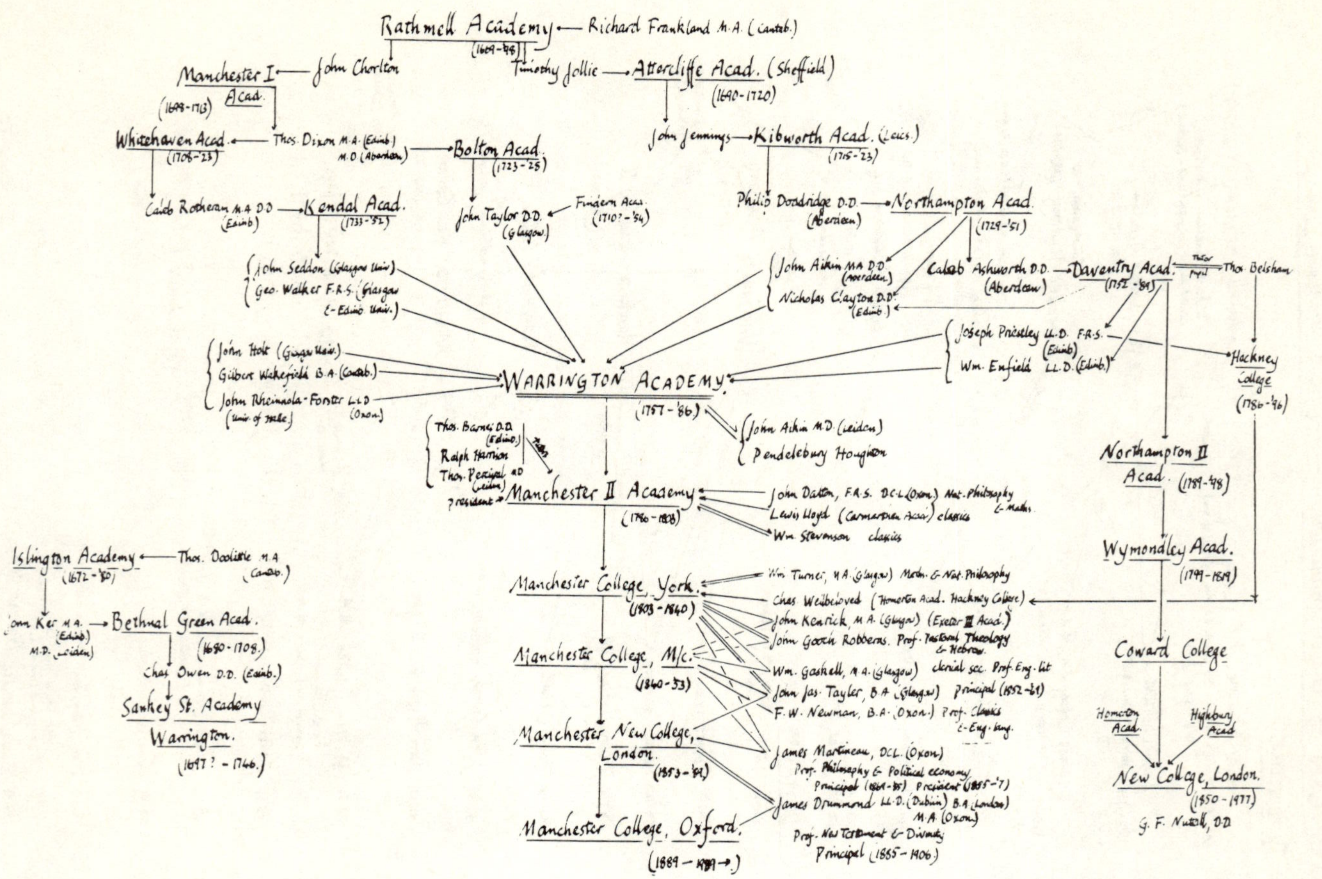
Rathmell Academy (1669-98)
Richard Frankland M.A. (Cantab.)
John Chorlton
Timothy Jollie
Attercliffe Acad. (Sheffield) (1690-1720)
Manchester I Acad. (1699-1713)
Whitehaven Acad. (1708-23)
Thos. Dixon M.A. (Edinb.) M.D. (Aberdeen)
Bolton Acad. (1723-25)
John Jennings
Kibworth Acad. (Leics.) (1715-23)
Philip Doddridge D.D. (Aberdeen)
Northampton Acad. (1729-'51)
Caleb Rotheram M.A. D.D. (Edinb.)
Kendal Acad. (1733-'52)
John Taylor D.D. (Glasgow)
Findern Acad. (1710?-'54)
John Seddon (Glasgow Univ.)
Geo. Walker F.R.S. (Glasgow & Edinb. Univ.)
John Aikin M.A. D.D. (Aberdeen)
Nicholas Clayton D.D. (Edinb.)
Caleb Ashworth D.D. (Aberdeen)
Daventry Acad. (1752-'89)
tutor
pupil
Thos. Belsham
Joseph Priestley LL.D. F.R.S. (Edinb.)
Wm. Enfield LL.D. (Edinb.)
Hackney College (1786-'96)
John Holt (Glasgow Univ.)
Gilbert Wakefield B.A. (Cantab.)
John Rheinhold-Forster LL.D (Oxon.) (Univ. of Halle)
WARRINGTON ACADEMY (1757-'86)
John Aikin M.D. (Leiden)
Pendlebury Houghton
Thos. Barnes D.D. (Edinb.)
Ralph Harrison
Thos. Percival M.D. (Leiden)
tutors
president
Manchester II Academy (1786-1803)
John Dalton, F.R.S. D.C.L. (Oxon.) Nat. Philosophy & Maths.
Lewis Loyd (Carmarthen Acad.) classics
Wm. Stevenson classics
Northampton II Acad. (1789-'98)
Wymondley Acad. (1799-1839)
Coward College
Homerton Acad.
Highbury Acad.
New College, London. (1850-1977)
G. F. Nuttall, D.D.
Manchester College, York. (1803-1840)
Wm. Turner, M.A. (Glasgow) Math. & Nat. Philosophy
Chas. Wellbeloved (Homerton Acad. Hackney College)
John Kenrick, M.A. (Glasgow) (Exeter II Acad.)
John Gooch Robberds. Prof. Pastoral Theology & Hebrew
Manchester College, M/c. (1840-53)
Wm. Gaskell, M.A. (Glasgow) clerical sec. Prof. Eng. Lit.
John Jas. Tayler, B.A. (Glasgow) Principal (1852-'69)
F. W. Newman, B.A. (Oxon.) Prof. Classics & Eng. Lang.
Manchester New College, London. (1853-'89)
James Martineau, D.C.L. (Oxon) Prof. Philosophy & Political economy Principal (1869-'85) President (1885-'7)
James Drummond LL.D. (Dublin) B.A. (London) M.A. (Oxon)
Prof. New Testament & Divinity Principal (1885-1906)
Manchester College, Oxford. (1889 →)
Islington Academy (1672-'80?)
Thos. Doolittle M.A. (Cantab.)
John Ker M.A. (Edinb.) M.D. (Leiden)
Bethnal Green Acad. (1680-1708.)
Chas. Owen D.D. (Edinb.)
Sankey St. Academy Warrington. (1697? - 1746.)

Chapter 4
WARRINGTON ACADEMY GROWTH AND PROMISE (1757 - 1770)

'Fearing it may prove a dry piece of disquisition, I have put a few pins and needles into it, just to keep attention awake.'
Alexander Gordon (1895)[1]

Warrington Academy was **'an entirely new foundation'** as Irene Parker said in 1914. But it did not spring from entirely fresh inspiration, as the rest of her statement seems to imply. It was built on firm academic foundations and on a tradition which had been around for nearly a century. It drew its tutors from a definite succession, as the last chapter has demonstrated.

The development was part of a straightforward evolutionary process, which was happening in parallel, but slightly different ways, at almost the same time, at Daventry. In the case of Daventry, as already seen, there was a simple and traditional succession from Northampton. But new features emerged. Mainly, these were the employment of several tutors to teach different groups of subjects, and a succession of tutors while the Academy lasted. Daventry also inherited the library, archives and apparatus from Doddridge's Academy, which passed back to Northampton in 1789, and onwards in time to New College, London,[2] just as Warrington inherited scientific apparatus from Kendal, which would in time pass on to Hackney, together with the accessions from Holt and Clayton, which will be mentioned later.

In the case of the new foundation at Warrington the development and tradition was very similar, but the manner of its birth was quite different. There was a deliberate pause for review of the situation, and quite thoughtful planning before the project was launched.

A major change had come in the political climate. Following the collapse of the 1745 uprising the threat of a Stuart restoration finally faded, and with it the harassment of dissenters also disappeared, although the Test Acts would remain on the Statute book until well into the next century (1828). Many of the non-conformist families were now well established in trade and industry. They were becoming people of consequence and wealth, and they wished to broaden their provisions for higher education.

However in the 1750s the situation for academies had become critical.[3] Doddridge had just died and a succession was not yet fully established. The following year Rotheram died and the Kendal Academy dissolved. In 1754 Dr. Latham followed, with the loss of Findern (near Derby) and available academy places in the provinces were becoming less and less.

David Jennings had advised Doddridge[4] that he should establish, not merely a seminary for non-conformist ministers, but provide education for other learned professions as well. Now it was being acknowledged that businessmen also needed a good education. As the first proposal for a new institution stated,[5]

> 'It is now become a general and just complaint that some Publick Provision is wanted for the education of young gentlemen, designed either for the learned professions or for Business...a Publick Academy conducted by a Number of Tutors . . .'

A circular published in 1754 stated,[6]

> 'It is well calculated for those that are to be engaged in a Commercial Life, as well as the Learned Professions; to give them some Knowledge of the more useful Branches of Literature; and to lead them to an early Acquaintance with and just concern for, the True Principles of Religion and Liberty, of which great interest they must in future life be the supporters.'

According to McLachlan however, although there was considerable lip service paid to these ideals, the financial support did not materialise. He writes of,[7]

> 'These men . . . of the day book and ledger, accustomed to casting balances respecting things tangible, (who) did not reckon that education of a public character, even when relating to the material not less than to the spiritual, could not like commerce, agriculture, banking and shipping be made to pay in pounds, shillings and pence.'

He makes it clear that without endowments the Academy was being built on shifting sands.

What these captains of industry and commerce did appreciate was that the universities, even if they had been freely accessible, were not providing anything like the standard of education which they had come to expect from the academies. Oxford and Cambridge were still in a phase of extraordinary decadence. Dr. Waterland's 'Advice to a Young Student',[8] republished at Oxford in 1755, recommended most of the old teachers, and the familiar arrangement of the Arts Course with its emphasis on Ciceronianism and disputations on subjects unrelated to life. Aristotle reigned supreme in Philosophy. Science was largely neglected, and exercises and examinations wore all the appearance of a solemn farce.

Early in the reign of George III a foreign visitor to Oxford witnessed a degree examination which filled him with amazement.[9] The examiner, candidate and others concerned passed the statutory time in perfect quiet, reading novels and other entertaining works. When Lord Eldon graduated there in 1770 he was asked only two questions: 'What is the Hebrew for the place of a skull? And, who founded University College?' By replying 'Golgotha and King Alfred' he satisfied the examiners. This bears an amazing resemblance to some late twentieth century popular television quiz shows, in which a winner for the 'goodies' on offer is a requisite for the entertainment of the mob. So questions must not be too searching.

At Cambridge no lecture was delivered by any Regius Professor of Modern History between 1725 and 1773. Mathematics held a commanding place, thanks to the influence of Isaac Newton, but few were attracted to study it.[10]

One of the most damning indictments comes from the pen of Edward Gibbon[11] who, as a Gentleman Commoner, was admitted to the Fellows' table at Magdalen College, Oxford in 1752. He says of the students there, 'From the toil of reading or thinking or writing they had absolved their conscience. Their conversation stagnated in a round of College business, Tory politics, personal stories and private scandal; their dull and deep potations excused the brisk intemperance of youth.'

Rev. John Seddon,[12] who followed Charles Owen in the ministry at Sankey Street Chapel, is a most significant figure in the foundation of the Academy at Warrington. A young man, just into his thirties when he arrived, he was full of energy, drive and enthusiasm. Born in Hereford, son of a dissenting minister who had been educated at Frankland's Academy; he himself was educated at Caleb Rotheram's Academy in Kendal, and then at Glasgow University. So he was no stranger to the North of England and its problems. He was undoubtedly inspired by the fact that he was following a minister who had conducted a successful academy of the older type for almost half a century.

Manchester and Liverpool were strongly in contention for the new project, and Ormskirk had some support from Liverpool as a compromise site. But Seddon's tireless campaigning and fund-raising, travelling extensively around the country for the purpose, almost certainly tipped the balance in favour of Warrington. According to Lucy Aikin, he 'did not scruple some stout puffing' on its behalf. McLachlan described him as a sort of Pooh Bah or 'Lord High Everything Else' in relation to the Academy. He was secretary to the trustees and attended all meetings of the tutors, so that he was in fact a liaison officer between the two, and all the business of the establishment passed through his hands.

Seddon not only wrote letters for the trustees, but he copied these laboriously in long hand into the minute book,[13] thus enlarging the record of what transpired. In all these ways he had a powerful role in shaping policy. He was appointed librarian and had full charge of the books. He also had pastoral care of a section of the student body living in his family home. He kept in close touch with the parents and guardians of his charges, and this role was extended after a few years when he was made rector, and thus responsible for the pastoral care of all the students.

His emerging career as a teacher[14] tends to be overlooked, but in the early years, when the staff was minimal, Seddon caused quite a furore, by presuming to give some lectures in Theology, greatly upsetting John Taylor who regarded this as his own inviolable preserve. Later, when Priestley retired, he joined the teaching staff again. He undertook lectures on the Philosophy of Language and Grammar, also Oratory, Poetry and History. He was not averse to critising Priestley and, as McLachlan tells us, he flattered himself on his own 'precision and perspicuity'.

He also ventured into the field of Divinity again, but now his senior was the much more tolerant Dr. Aikin. He lectured on Evidences of Christianity, Metaphysics, Morals and Logic, using the lecture notes of Doddridge, which were used as a textbook at Warrington just then. Again, he was quite prepared to argue against this authority when he saw fit. McLachlan applauds this tendency as illustrating 'the method of unfettered inquiry in vogue at Warrington'. It is interesting to speculate how his career might have evolved had he lived longer.

In addition John Seddon was one of the main founders, in the year after the Academy itself started, of the **Warrington Public Library**,[15] of which he became the first President. This circulating library formed the nucleus of what was eventually to become the town's local history and reference library, with its unique collection of books reflecting the activities of academic tutors and their friends; many of the volumes being printed in Warrington at Eyre's Press.

To complete the picture, Seddon played a leading role in the affairs of the Provincial Meeting of Ministers. He was also a founder and first secretary of the Widows Fund Association, a mutual benefit society for the support of ministers' widows.

Initial meetings of the society, established to promote the proposed Academy, were held in Manchester at Cross Street Chapel, and almost certainly at other venues around the country. It seems remarkable that minutes refer to 'The Society' but it is not given a name. The initial proposal of July 1754 apparently emanated from Manchester.[16] In June 1757 a formal meeting of Trustees took place at Warrington, and minutes in the Academy's book are recorded for the first time. Here it is stated, 'That for the present and as a temporary settlement, Warrington is the most convenient situation for the Academy' – a prophetic statement.

The Officers elected were:–

President of the Society – Lord Willoughby de Parham (Hugh, fifteenth Baron).

Vice-President – John Lees of Manchester (who later changed his name to become John Carill Worsley).

Treasurer – Arthur Heywood of Liverpool.

Secretary – Rev. John Seddon.

Lord Willoughby, whose family seat was in Lancashire at Rivington, was the representative of the last of the Presbyterian noble families. He was thought to be quite a catch. The somewhat obsequious invitation to him said,[17] 'Our gentlemen seemed very desir-

Warrington Academy building at Bridgefoot 1986, following renovation.

ous to avail themselves of your Lordship's name at the head of the design. They think it will give them an importance they cannot otherwise have . . .' In the event they can only have been disappointed because, apart from his name and a modest subscription, he contributed little. He seems never to have attended a meeting of trustees. George Willoughby, a distant relation, and destined to become the seventeenth Baron, (last of the line) came later from London to be educated at Warrington Academy.[18] When Hugh Willoughby died in 1765 he was succeeded as President by John Lees, who took a much more active part in the affairs of the Academy.

A home was found for the establishment in an existing house at Bridgefoot. This was built by William Middlehurst of Latchford as a town house, and first occupied sometime between 1735 and 1740. It afforded ample provision for the Academy in its early years, and in that period little thought seems to have been given to future accommodation if it grew as was hoped. Certainly there is no comment in the trustees' minutes.

Rev. William Turner,[19] a pupil of the Academy and its first historian, refers to this first home as 'a range of buildings . . . to which was attached a considerable extent of garden and ground, and a handsome terrace walk on the banks of the Mersey; possessing altogether, a respectable collegiate appearance.'

The first reference to an accommodation problem comes in the Trustees' Annual Report for 1761 where it is stated, 'The trustees have found themselves unkindly treated by the proprietor of the houses (there were in fact two, semi-detached) where the Academy has been hitherto fixed, in being refused a lease and having their rent unreasonably advanced. *A number of them, at their own private expense,* have this summer erected two convenient houses for the accommodation of the tutors, and large enough for the reception of several boarders, to which will be added before the end of the year, a Common Hall, with proper apartments for the several classes where lectures are to be given, and *a Public Library.*'

These buildings were off Buttermarket Street in a cul-de-sac behind the Friends' Meeting House, which became known as Academy Place. In the second half of the nineteenth century the Common Hall was demolished and a thoroughfare completed between Buttermarket Street and Mersey Street, to be known as Academy Street. The last remnant, the tutors' house, first occupied by Priestley and his family, on the east side of the entrance, was finally demolished in 1978 when the highway was widened as part of the inner ring road.

The tutors who were allocated the houses in Academy Place[20] were expected to take students as boarders 'at a rate of £15 p.a. for those who had two months vacation and £18 for those who had none, but these terms did not include candles, fire and washing, nor the luxury of tea!' Even with this addition to their remuneration of £100 p.a. it could hardly be said that the tutors were overpaid.

This development was remarkable in two respects. It was the first purposely designed range of buildings in the history of the Dissenter academies, and it was the result of private enterprise, built by a number of the trustees with their own money.

In 1762 the minutes of the sixth general meeting of the trustees record that it was 'agreed the Society do immediately purchase the said building and make it the property of the Academy.'

The same report mentions that 'every student upon his Admission gives a sum not less than half a guinea to the library,' thus continuing the tradition established by Doddridge at Northampton. In 1770 the fee was raised to one guinea, and this income was used for the purchase of books.

In 1766 the Annual Report mentions the sizable debt incurred by erecting the buildings, but states that with considerable benefactions, and as a result of 'little savings' (good housekeeping), this had been reduced from £1700 to £700. As soon as the debt was discharged the buildings were to become the property of the Academy, and then the plan could be finished by building apartments for the reception of students.

By 1767 the establishment was obviously considered to be on a sound footing because the tutors were requested to choose a rector. Their choice, not surprisingly, was John Seddon, who, about the same time, was appointed as a tutor to teach History in place of Priestley, who had just left. The report for that year also mentions that subscriptions were coming in satisfactorily, and there was a decision to carry on with the building programme.

The next report states that a range of apartments with twenty-six rooms had now been completed. These were single rooms for the more affluent, and perhaps also the more studious, with double rooms to be shared by others. All students could now be accommodated, so there would no longer be a need for them to be boarded out in the town. They were to reside in these rooms, or in the house of Mr. Holt or Mr John Rigby's house 'within the verge of the Academy' (at the rear of the new block). It went on to state that, 'Mr. and Mrs. Rigby are chosen as proper persons to conduct the commons, and furnish the apartments of the students.' In other words they were the housekeepers. They were related to Dr. John Taylor, the first principal tutor, who had died in 1761.

The buildings of the Academy now formed a quite impressive group. The entrance, with handsome wrought iron gate and railings, was flanked by the two tutors' houses (other tutors lived elsewhere in the town). Between these, one looked in upon the main academic block, of goodly proportions, with a clock above the main doorway, and crowned with a small cupola. Set back slightly on the west side was the student residence block. The small quadrangle thus formed was open on the east side, and as late as 1780 the trustees were determined to complete the design by building on that side and closing the gap. But alas this was not to be.

All in all this modest but dignified complex had something of the atmosphere and appearance of one of the smaller Oxbridge colleges. In 1852, when the first Ordnance Survey Map of Warrington was published, these buildings were still intact, and a detailed ground plan appears on that map.

Warrington Academy had many problems and difficulties in the years ahead, but it started with undoubted advantages. In the words of McLachlan,[21]

> (it) 'was established as an independent academical institution. It enjoyed no charter, or state support, but, like the private academies after 1689, it was also free from state control, and, unlike Northampton and others, was born too late to suffer from ecclesiastical interference, or from political reaction such as was expressed in the Schism Act, which temporarily closed the doors of many academies. It had . . . its own trustees, subscribers and management committee, and was the earliest and most important example of the institutional type of academy.'
>
> 'No previous academy was so oecumenical in character. Students, though never numerous, came from every part of the British Isles, from the West Indies, and the American colonies. They included a few sons of titled persons, and many more of commercial magnates, professional men, tradesmen, and impoverished dissenting divines. Never previously in non-conformist seminaries, nor in English universities since the Middle Ages, had there been such a mingling of student types as were assembled from time to time at Warrington.'
>
> ....
>
> 'As Warrington was open to youths with secular, no less than those with religious aims in life, without respect to race or creed, its tutors were not drawn exclusively from the ranks of dissenting ministers, as with a few exceptions, they had been in earlier academies, especially those devoted to the supply of ministers.'
>
> 'For an excellent practical reason, then, Warrington was altogether free from religious tests for teachers and pupils alike, the first institution making so wide an appeal to

boast such freedom, *after heresy had raised its head in non-conformity,* (sic) until the rise of the modern university colleges.'

Tutors.

When the Academy was launched in 1757 it was intended to have three tutors. But in the event, with only five students enrolled, the trustees settled for two. **John Taylor, D.D.**[22] was the first, and in the years remaining to him, the principal tutor, responsible for the course in Divinity. A native of Lancaster, educated at Bolton and Findern Academies, he was a renowned scriptural scholar, whose greatest work, a Hebrew concordance, had just been published. His teaching experience, however, was far behind him. His first ministry was near Lincoln, where, to supplement an income of £33 p.a. he took boys 'to table and teach'. But for want of a fire in his study he was, in after life, crippled with rheumatism.

Taylor launched his course at Warrington Academy with a great flourish, perhaps his most significant contribution, which was to set an academic style for the establishment throughout its life and thereafter for its successors. This was '**his charge**' to the young men embarking on their studies. The thinking was not unique, because similar ideas had been expressed at other academies, but it crystallised and formalised them in a way that would never be forgotten. It runs as follows:[23]

> 'I do solemnly charge you, in the name of the God of Truth, and of Our Lord Jesus Christ, who is the Way the Truth and the Life, and before whose judgement seat you must in no long time appear:
>
> *First.* That in all your studies and inquiries of a religious nature, present or future, you do constantly, carefully, impartially and conscientiously, attend to evidence as it lies in the Holy Scriptures, or in the nature of things and the dictates of reason, cautiously guarding against the sallies of imagination and the fallacy of ill-grounded conjecture.
>
> *Second.* That you admit, embrace or assent to no principle or sentiment, by me taught or advanced, but only so far as it shall appear to you to be supported and justified by proper evidence from Revelation, or in the reason of things.
>
> *Third.* That if at any time hereafter any principle or sentiment by me taught or advanced, or by you admitted or

> embraced, shall upon impartial and faithful examination, appear to you to be dubious or false, you either suspect or totally reject such principle or sentiment.
>
> *Fourth.* That you keep your mind always open to evidence; that you labour to banish from your breast all prejudice, prepossession and party zeal; that you study to live in peace and love with all your fellow christians; and that you steadily assert for yourself, and freely allow to others, the inalienable rights of judgement and conscience.'

Could there be a nobler or more challenging statement of the true principles of education as distinct from learning by rote? The sad fact, however, is that from early on Taylor himself did not adhere to these principles. Very soon he found himself at odds with John Seddon, with some of whose theological opinions he was not in agreement. They also differed about prayer and about the style of 'The New Liturgy' on which the younger man was engaged and which was published in Liverpool in 1762. Seddon, possibly because the staff was small, and also because of his own intense interest in the whole project, undertook, apparently on his own initiative, and with a degree of insensitivity, to deliver some lectures to students. Taylor resented this. He seemed to regard Seddon as a cocky young upstart who had no right to be expressing contrary opinions to *his* students, thus ignoring the contradiction with his own statement. This is in contrast with the cut and thrust already noted in the contemporary Academy at Daventry.

The difference between these two men rapidly became a major crisis[24] which was to exercise the Board of Trustees. These, after careful consideration, came down on the side of their secretary.[25] Taylor was very hurt and quite voluble in his complaints, and not long after he died. Unfortunately, it was not only he himself, but also his numerous supporters and admirers throughout the land who shared this sense of outrage. Many of these withdrew support and remained implacable enemies of the Academy at Warrington throughout its existence, even after Seddon's own untimely end in 1770.

This was a tragic and savage wound, which in retrospect was quite avoidable. Seddon, the trustees and others, should have appreciated that they were dealing with an elderly man in poor health, who was also concerned about his wife's ill-health. His own longstanding rheumatism was a painful and disabling condition, probably with many sleepless nights and other problems which come with age. It is likely that the rheumatic disease had affected his heart, thus bringing on sudden failure and death in his sleep.

A proper appraisal could have avoided the immediate, as well as the long term consequences of this rift. Reasonable tact with a modicum of compassion would probably have assuaged the old man and made his final days a lot happier. But such virtues are not always to be found in academic circles. Instead, he was made thoroughly miserable, feeling quite misunderstood, and the memory of him in the years ahead was that of a sort of bogeyman who had soured relationships in a most damaging manner for the young Academy.

With hindsight we might wonder why Dr. Aikin, who was a notable man of peace, did not manage to promote harmony between his two colleagues. But people living through a situation do not always see the issues as clearly as those who can stand back and make their assessment without the current emotion. Perhaps Aikin did try. Perhaps his efforts were frustrated by Taylor himself. Perhaps, at the time, this cantankerous old man seemed little more than a tiresome nuisance to those about him, who had to endure the problems he generated. Perhaps it was hoped that time would heal the rift. But suddenly Dr. Taylor was dead, and it was too late. It is significant that he was not buried in the Sankey Street Chapel but in Chowbent at Atherton, north-west of Manchester, not far from his Alma Mater, where he had probably preached from time to time.

The second tutor appointed with Taylor was **John Holt**,[26] a graduate of Glasgow University, who in earlier years had been a minister at Lancaster, and then for many years had kept a large mathematical and commercial school at Kirkdale near Liverpool, where many Lancashire merchants were educated. He was responsible for the teaching of Mathematics and Science for fifteen years until his death in 1772.

He was obviously a solid and reliable member of staff, who made his home in one of the new houses into which the Academy moved in 1762, and where he took students in to board with his family. It is hard to assess his character and personality. Mrs. Barbauld later referred to him as 'a sort of reasoning automaton whose soul was absorbed by his Science.' But Seddon, in his letter conveying the trustees' invitation to him to join the staff refers to 'your great abilities, your very amiable character . . . and the honourable and affectionate manner in which your pupils have ever mentioned your name.' Various stories are recorded which portray him as an odd eccentric. McLachlan relates how, 'Even in his will his mathematical mania found scope for exercise, and his estate was divided amongst his relatives in strict proportion to their nearness of kin to him, without mentioning a single name, even that of his wife,[a] their shares ranging from "sixty-four parts" to "one part".'

The first collection of scientific apparatus which the Academy possessed was Holt's, and Priestley acknowledges an indebtedness to him in the preface to his 'History of Electricity'. It was to be a significant feature among the teaching staff that they were ever eager to learn from one another.

The second year brought the number of students up to twenty-three, and a third tutor was appointed. This was **John Aikin**,[27] who came from Kibworth and who has already been mentioned. The arrival of the Aikin family was a most significant and felicitous event for the Academy, making for great stability after the unhappy events already mentioned. Aikin was appointed to the tutorship in 'Belles Lettres' (polite literature). But after only three years, when Taylor died, he moved over to Divinity. Initially he had experience of teaching for a short time as an assistant to Philip Doddridge at Northampton. Then he had his own primary school at Kibworth. He was a highly valued teacher and a good scholar, regarded universally as a friend and mentor. He was also a benign disciplinarian who helped the establishment through many difficulties with students in the years ahead.

Young John Aikin, although but eleven years old when they arrived, was immediately entered as a student of the Academy, probably the youngest ever. In spite of his tender age he settled well to his studies and made good progress in the normal time. Aikin's daughter, **Anna Laetitia**, had been a pupil in her father's school for boys at Kibworth, which was a source of some anxiety to her somewhat straitlaced mother. But there was no question of her continuing to have a formal education in this more senior all-male establishment. She was fifteen when they arrived at Warrington, but it is obvious from a variety of evidence that her learning had not ceased. Undoubtedly she had further private tuition from her father, but she also learned many things from other tutors with whom she had a friendly relationship, especially Dr. Priestley who was the next tutor to be appointed. She had a competent grasp of Classical Literature, History and Theology. She was very much au fait with English Literature and had knowledge of other European languages. She also had a useful smattering of scientific knowledge. In time she became a well known writer in both prose and verse, and had a career as a primary school teacher

---

a *Holt's will does in fact specifically mention his wife – copy in W'gton library.*

for a number of years at Palgrave in Suffolk, after her marriage to the Rev. Rochemont Barbauld.

Aikin, unlike some of the other tutors, did not live in the Academy, and because of his indifferent health he was not expected to take in students to board. He took a large house nearby in Buttermarket Street, and this homestead played an important role in both the social and cultural life of the Academy. The Aikins' hospitality was renowned. John Aikin had graduated as an M.A. from King's College, Aberdeen in 1737, and after he had been at Warrington for some sixteen years that University conferred upon him a D.D. in recognition of his outstanding achievement as a Divinity tutor.

Thomas Barnes, an old pupil of Aikin, said of him in later years,[28] 'He was uncommonly revered by all who knew him, for the wonderful extent of his knowledge, for the mild dignity of his character and for the various excellencies which adorned the Scholar, the Tutor and the Man.' Another contemporary, Andrew Kippis, said of him, 'As a lecturer he was perhaps never excelled; this is the testimony that has been given of him by all who had the advantage of being his pupils.'

One of those who knew him in his last years was William Turner, and his assessment is most revealing,[29]

> 'This excellent man lived always in perfect harmony with his colleagues, and with the trustees, and on all occasions acted as a general friend and a bond of union. His influence over the students, which was very great, arose not merely from the excellence of his instructions, but from the kind concern which he took in their welfare, and the affectionate interest with which he always tempered the authority which appeared in his private advice, or, where he saw it necessary, his reproofs and remonstrances. Being, of course, constantly spoken of in the language of warm attachment and reverence by the students who were his immediate pupils, he became an object of veneration bordering upon awe among those who were not; and though his delicate state of health[30] prevented his frequent personal intercourse with the students at large, and absolutely precluded his taking part in the ordinary routine of academical discipline, yet this circumstance gave additional weight to his authority when circumstances occurred that called for his interference; which was always exercised after a previous cool, clear-sighted investigation, which put him in possession of the whole case: after which his decision was made with promptitude and firmness, and the measures dictated by it were

declared and executed, with a dignity and propriety peculiar to himself, and always perfectly efficient.'

Joseph Priestley – statue in Priestley College, Warrington.

Betsy Rodgers[a] throws further light on his limitations when she comments that[31] 'Aikin's delicate health and his tendency to asthma made him avoid lectures (as already he had had to abandon preaching) and more and more his teaching resembled a seminar'. This fortuitous circumstance was just one more factor which went to mould the distinctive academic style of the Warrington establishment.

When Aikin was first appointed another candidate to be considered was **Joseph Priestley,**[32] but he was turned down on account of his youth and inexperience, together with the fact that he had something of a stammer. The trustees could not ascertain how severe this was as he was far away in Suffolk. However, three years later, on the death of Taylor, his turn came, and this time the selectors had no doubt. By then he was minister, not too far off, at Nantwich, where he had a school for boys and girls. So they now had some opportunity of getting to know his worth.

Priestley became the most famous of all the tutors and did more to give the Academy its unique status than anybody else. The leading academies aspired to provide university learning, and the decadence of Oxbridge, previously noted, made it easier for them to claim this. But there is more to a true university than merely an establishment in which to learn; both staff and students should be probing and exploring; pushing back the frontiers of knowledge. Taylor's programme already suggested such a dimension at Warrington Academy, but it was Priestley who brought it to fruition.

It comes as a surprise to many who know of Priestley mainly, or even solely, as a scientist, to know that Science was never anything but a hobby with him, and that he was primarily a minister. In religion he was always 'heterodox'. He was brought up by an aunt who was a pillar of their local chapel in Yorkshire. They were Calvinist, and her home was always open to visiting as well as local ministers. She appears to have been remarkably liberal and tolerant because he tells us in his autobiography that some of these visitors

---

a *A descendant of the Aikin's*

were deemed heretical but had a considerable influence on his own views.

Before he left home he had wished to be 'admitted a communicant in the congregation which (he) had always attended.'[33] The minister, whose views were similar to those of his aunt, was agreeable; but the elders refused him because at their interrogation they found some of his views were not acceptable to them.

His younger brother Timothy, ever 'orthodox', went to the Independent academy at Heckmondwike (Yorkshire) and became a Congregational minister. Jack Lindsay mentions[34] the funeral sermon he preached when news was received of his brother's death in far off Pennsylvania, which mingled 'family pride and a conviction of Joseph's damnation'. Such is man's presumption to upstage God in the matter of final judgement!

By the time that Joseph Priestley arrived at Warrington he had already been a minister at two places: the first in Suffolk, the second in Nantwich. But he was not yet ordained. He was at his most docile just at this point, perhaps because of his new appointment, but also it has been hinted because of his impending marriage. So, ordained he was.

Priestley married Mary Wilkinson, daughter of Isaac Wilkinson, the great iron-master of Wrexham, whom he had met when her young brother was a pupil of his at Nantwich. Mary was an

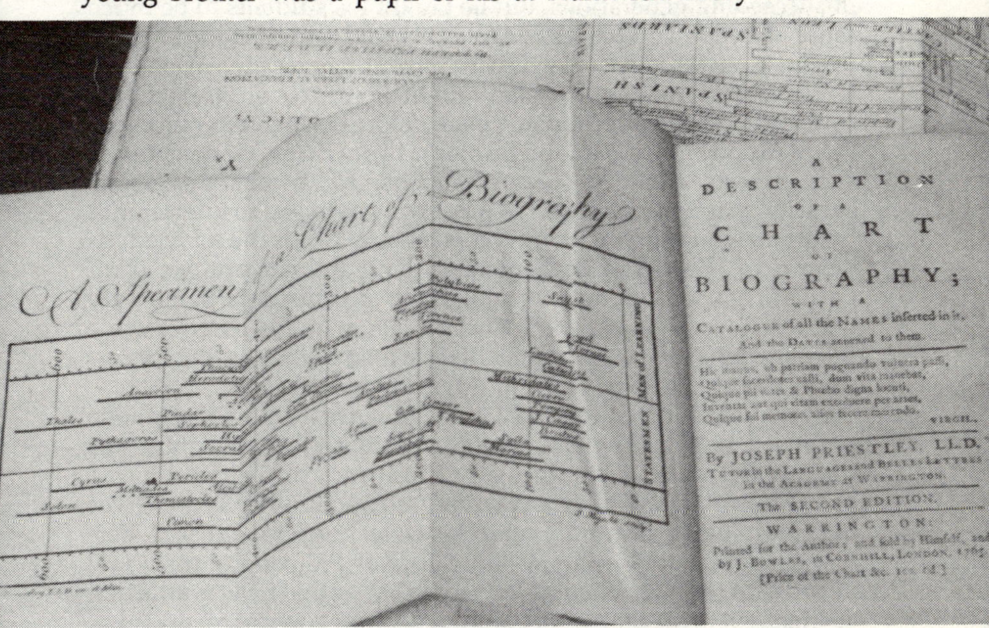

Priestley's Chart of Biography printed in Warrington at Eyres Press from the library of Manchester College, Oxford.

excellent wife and a great support to him throughout her life. He also had considerable financial backing from her family which facilitated his many unique scientific projects in the years ahead.

An outstanding feature of Priestley's career at Warrington Academy was that he did not consider himself in any way limited by his rather narrow brief. His active and fertile mind moved in many directions, and his eventual list of publications is breathtaking in its expanse. In the language and literature department to which he was appointed there are works on grammar, oratory and criticism, which are still quoted in specialist works on English Language even today.[35]

He published **'Observations on Education'** closely allied with several works on **History** which quite revolutionised this as a discipline. A comment of Gordon's[36] neatly expresses Priestley's highly individual approach to his task and the opportunities which he so clearly perceived. He said,

> 'At Warrington . . . they set him to teach rhetoric; but he struck out a line of his own, converting a tutorship in the *belles lettres* into a chair of constitutional history.'

Popular History came packaged as the fossilised propaganda of deceased autocrats dressed in romantic garb, to the utter confusion of succeeding generations. But he taught his students to be much more objective and professional in this study; they should look at original sources and hard evidence rather than merely accept these stilted commentaries. He also taught them to consider closely constitution and government,[37] even before his famous contemporaries Adam Smith, Edmund Burke and Tom Paine. He considered such aspects as the proper recompense for labour, and social security, in a basic manner. He was firmly opposed to interference by the state in religion. Some years later, at Leeds, he advised his hearers to, 'Respect a parliamentary king and cheerfully pay all parliamentary taxes; but have nothing to do with a parliamentary religion, or a parliamentary God.' As soon as his lectures were published they were recommended by John Symonds, the Professor of Modern History at Cambridge,[38] to his students.

Even more surprisingly, he was to influence the Roman Catholic seminary at Douai, where a reorganisation of the syllabus was undertaken in the 1780s during the Presidency of William Gibson, on the model of 'Priestley's Warrington Academy.'[39] Gibson gives the credit for this inspiration[40] to his colleague Father Joseph Berrington,[41] who had occupied the Chair of Philosophy for a few years prior to 1772, when he left Douai. After that he was attached as Chaplain to the Stapleton family at Carlton Towers in Yorkshire. It was probably at that time, in 1772-3, that he first met Priestley, who was then at Leeds. In 1776 Berrington was corresponding with

Priestley on the topic of 'Materialism and Hartley's Theory of the Human Mind', by which time each would have been acquainted with details of the other's academic career. Although they disagreed on Hartley's Necessarian Philosophy, Berrington obviously appreciated Priestley's general Philosophy of Education. Milburn[42] describes Berrington as 'a priest of known liberal tendencies'.

Priestley wrote constantly on Theology; before,during and after his years at Warrington. These works now have a vèry limited interest except to people of his own persuasion, but again it is worthy of note how broad were his sympathies, and liberal his attitude to others with whom he was in basic disagreement. He was never in sympathy with Rome and in 1770, writing from Leeds to his friend Theophilus Lindsey,[43] at that time Rector of Catterick, he replied to a query about Papists in his area, saying ' . . . nor, to my knowledge, did I ever converse with any papist in my life. We were brought up in a thorough abhorrence and contempt of them.' Yet in 1780, following the Gordon riots, he published anonymously a pamphlet[44] appealing to his Protestant fellow-countrymen for toleration. By then he had conversed with at least two Papists, because in his scientific studies he had been actively collaborating with the Abbé Boscovich,[45] a Jesuit and Physicist living in France, whose international reputation was such that he was elected a Fellow of the Royal Society.

Priestley was not engaged as a scientist at Warrington, but this is not to say that he did not pursue the subject actively at that time. It had been studied at earlier academies under the label of 'Natural Philosophy', a term which, though accurate, will be unfamiliar to many modern scientists. By then however Physics and Chemistry were beginning to be disentangled as separate disciplines.

Priestley, at Nantwich, had introduced his pupils to some basic Physics, his equipment including an air pump with which he encouraged them to demonstrate experiments to their parents and friends. The air pump was used mainly to demonstrate animal respiration, and such an 'Experiment with an Air Pump' was beautifully illustrated some years later by Joseph Wright of Derby in a painting which now hangs in the Tate Gallery. The scientist giving the demonstration is said to be Warltire, a colleague of, and collaborator with, Priestley at that time.

His first scientific publications were on Physics, when he was at the Academy. He was introduced through Seddon to members of the Royal Society, and it was Benjamin Franklin, already a Fellow, who prompted him to write 'A History of Electricity'.[46] This he did by consulting what literature was available, and also by devising original experiments of his own to check some of the statements he encountered. This work, together with the prompting of Thomas Percival, the Academy's first student, then in London, and an amazingly influential young man who had made powerful connections, persuaded the Royal Society to elect Priestley a Fellow. Around the same time the University of Edinburgh honoured him with its LL.D. in recognition of his work on the '**Chart of History**',[47] again through the agency of the same Percival. Another published study was on '**Vision, Light, and Colour**',[48] and by 1767 Priestley was able to write that,[49]

> 'Hitherto philosophy has been chiefly conversant about the more sensible properties of bodies; electricity, together with chymistry, and the doctrine of light and colour, seems to be giving us an inlet into their internal structure, on which their sensible properties depend. By pursuing this new light therefore, the bounds of natural science may possibly be extended, beyond what we can now form an idea of. New worlds may open to our view, and the glory of the great Sir Isaac Newton himself, and all his contemporaries be eclipsed, by a new set of philosophers, in a quite new field of speculation.'

Priestley himself was a leader among this new set of philosophers. It was not until the next generation that John Dalton would propound the atomic theory, but, in ways, Priestley and others like Boscovich were ahead of this, because although they did not know it as something that would be confirmed, their speculations were leading on to concepts of particulate matter at the sub-atomic level. On one occasion, musing on these problems he wrote,[50]

> 'What peculiar excellence is there in those particles of matter which compose my body, more than those which compose the table on which I write . . . if I knew they were instantly . . . to change places, I do not think it would give me any concern.'

This speculation might well be described as a theory of transubstantiation, although Priestley might jib at the terminology! He is disarmingly frank when he addresses himself to the problems of the experimental scientist, adopting the role of speculative philosopher as he contemplates:[51]

> ' . . . the force of prejudice which, unknown to ourselves, biases not only our *judgements,* properly so called, but even the perceptions of our senses; for we may take a maxim so strongly for granted that the plainest evidence of sense will not entirely change, and often hardly modify, our persuasions; and *the more ingenious a man is, the more effectually he is entangled in his errors,* his ingenuity

only helping to deceive himself by evading the force of truth.'

This foreshadows the problem which would be his own in later years, in which he stubbornly clung to the notion of phlogiston. Lavoisier could appreciate Priestley's great discovery in a positive fashion, which led him to name the new gas, oxygen, whilst the discoverer himself was still stuck with the negative concept of 'dephlogisticated air', and hence lost some of the credit for being first in the field.

When he arrived at Warrington Priestley was very much aware of his ignorance on the subject of Chemistry. The way in which he tackled this problem is typical of the man. He persuaded the trustees to engage Matthew Turner of Liverpool, through the good offices of Thomas Bentley.[a] Turner came to the Academy on a part-time contract for a couple of years to lecture on the subject and demonstrate experiments. Turner's most enthusiastic student was none other than Joseph Priestley.

From his second year and the time of his marriage Priestley occupied one of the new tutors houses flanking the entrance to Academy Place, and as with Holt on the other side, students were taken in to board in the Priestleys' home. Out at the back and quite detached from the main residence was a small building which was used as study and laboratory. Something of the kind was a feature of Priestley's home wherever he lived thenceforward, because his experiments in Chemistry could be hazardous, with a constant risk of explosion and fire. However the only fire recorded, which caused the total destruction of his home as well as the outbuilding, was years later in Birmingham,[52] during the years of the French Revolution, when the 'Church and King' mob rioted on the second anniversary of the fall of the Bastille. At Warrington there was no such damage, either accidental or deliberate.

From this time onwards Priestley's main scientific interest was with pneumatic chemistry or '**Different Kinds of Air**'[53] as he labels the topic in his own book on the subject. It has been assumed and stated that this work did not progress while he was at Warrington. T.E. Thorpe, writing in 1906,[54] records 'a local tradition that an adjoining building was used by him as a laboratory, although it is difficult to find any grounds for the belief'.

Thorpe, and other writers, have failed to spot clear evidence of the 'grounds for the belief' because it comes from unexpected sources on the literary rather than the scientific side. Dr. Kendrick

---

a *Thos. Bentley, the future partner of Josiah Wedgwood, was a trustee of the academy.*

in his 'Mornings Ramble in Old Warrington'[55] describes 'a small house' behind Priestley's residence which 'was used by him as a laboratory for chemical and electrical experiments, and it is not improbable that he here made his earliest discoveries of the nature of oxygen . . . and other gases.' Kendrick lived but a short distance away, and was familiar with these buildings throughout his life. He was also in touch with Lucy Aikin, who was a direct link with the people of the Academy. He goes on to quote the poems of her Aunt Laetitia, which throw so much extra light on the subject, and which Lucy had edited in the posthumous 'Works'.

Anna Laetitia Aikin, his fellow tutor's daughter, was greatly influenced by Priestley and certainly knew of his scientific work. In teaching English Priestley was accustomed to put his students through their paces by getting them to write verse; not, as he said, to make poets of them, but to improve their prose style. He claims it was this influence which launched Laetitia as one of the foremost women poets of her day. Her first book of verse was published in 1773 and contains a poem entitled **'The Mouse's Petition'**. This is a whimsical plea from a little mouse caught alive in a trap, begging for its life to be spared. It is a small gem in its own right, but its particular interest here lies in a footnote which was added to the second edition, in which the poetess reveals that the incident concerned a mouse which she found in a trap in Priestley's study. She knew the nature of his experiments and so wrote this piece to tease him.[56]

'O hear a pensive prisoner's prayer,
    For liberty that sighs;
And never let thine heart be shut
    Against the wretch's cries!

For here forlorn and sad I sit,
    Within the wiry grate;
And tremble at the approaching morn,
    Which brings impending fate.

If e'er thy breast with freedom glowed,
    And spurned a tyrant's chain,
Let not thy strong oppressive force
    A free-born mouse detain!

....

The cheerful light, *the vital air*,
    Are blessings widely given;
Let Nature's commoners enjoy

The common gifts of Heaven.'

In his own work Priestley discusses the question, 'Whether an animal will live in any kind of air', and describes his experiments, 'I generally make use of mice for this purpose.' He placed them on a platform over water in a small, closed, glass vessel . . . 'in this vessel a mouse will live for twenty minutes or half an hour . . . it is most convenient to catch the mice in small wire traps . . . (and) . . . pass them through water into the vessel which contains the air.'[57]

Another of the poems is '**An Inventory of the Furniture in Dr. Priestley's Study**'.[58] This is a marvellous snapshot by a friend who obviously appreciates the full and broad range of his activities.

'A map of every country known,
With not a foot of land his own.
A list of folks that kicked the dust
On this poor globe, from Ptol. the First;
He hopes, – indeed it is but fair, –
Some day to get a corner there.
A group of all the British kings,
Fair emblem! on a packthread swings.
The Fathers, ranged in goodly row,
A decent, venerable show,

....

A Juvenal to hunt for mottos;
And Ovid's tales of nymphs and grottos.
The meek-robed lawyers, all in white;
Pure as the lamb, – at least, to sight.
A shelf of bottles, jar and phial
By which the rogues he can defy all, –
All filled with lightening keen and genuine,[a]
And many a little imp he'll pen you in;
Which like Le Sage's sprite, let out,
Among the neighbours makes a rout,
Brings down the lightning on their houses,
And kills their geese and frights their spouses.[b]

---

a *Electrical batteries*

b *From Benjamin Franklin's 1752 experiments with kite and lightning conductors. Franklin was a friend and associate of Priestley who prompted him to write his 'History of Electricity'*

A rare thermometer, by which
He settles, to the nicest pitch,
The just degrees of heat, to raise
Sermons, or politics, or plays.
Papers and books, a strange mixed olio,
From shilling touch to pompous folio;
Answer, remark, reply, rejoinder,
Fresh from the mint, all stamped and coined here;

....

New books, like new-born infants, stand,
Waiting the printer's clothing hand; –
Others, a motley ragged brood,
Their limbs unfashioned all, and rude,
Like Cadmus' half-formed men appear;
One rears a helm, one lifts a spear,

....

And all, like controversial writing,
Were born with teeth, and sprung up fighting.

"But what is this," I hear you cry,
"Which saucily provokes my eye?" –
A thing unknown, without a name,
Born of the air and doomed to flame.'

So, what is this thing unknown? – perhaps hydrogen ('inflammable air') which was isolated before oxygen – 'born of the air and doomed to flame'.

Years later she wrote a moving poem addressed to Priestley in his final years, when he was a political refugee forced into exile in distant Pennsylvania. In the final verse she looks forward,[59]

'To the slow payment of that distant day, –
If distant, – when thy name to Freedom's joined,
Shall meet the thanks of a regenerate land.'

Many may believe that the land was regenerated in the nineteenth century at the time of the great Reform Act, soon after Anna Laetitia died. But has Priestley been reinstated to his proper place in the annals of that land? – Not yet!

Every self-respecting university today has its 'University Press', from which issue the learned contributions of its scholars. Warrington Academy had a great outpouring of excellent literature. Priestley's works were numerous, but he was not alone. There were other tutors and former students publishing, as well as more distant friends who were drawn into the Warrington net. They were fortunate in that there was a good printing works in the town – **Eyres' Press.** Many of its books are still to be found in libraries, both public and private; especially in the Warrington Academy library itself which reposes at Manchester College, Oxford; The Warrington Reference Library; Dr. Williams' library in London, and other specialised collections.

William Eyres printed a catalogue[60] for the Academy library, and also such items as charts and maps. Among works printed by friends of the Academy were Thomas Pennant's 'Tour in Scotland' and his 'British Zoology', William Roscoe's 'Mount Pleasant', and best known of all – John Howard's 'State of the Prisons' – the great classic of penal reform. John Watson's 'History of the Ancient Earls of Warren' was described by Gilbert Wakefield as 'perhaps the most accurate specimen of typography ever produced by any press.' And John Aikin's 'Tacitus' was described by Edward Harwood as 'a beautifully printed book'. A copy was advertised by Sanders of Oxford just a few years ago, the notice referring to Eyres as 'an under-rated printer'.

Eyres Press, Horsemarket Street, Warrington ("The Warrington University Press").

In the 1760s Warrington Academy enjoyed its most settled and fruitful years, described by Henry Bright[61] as its 'Golden Age'. On Saturdays the tutors, their students, members of their families and visiting friends used to come together to hear students read from their compositions, make speeches, and perform scenes from plays. At the end of each session there were more formal academic exercises, but on the same lines. The tutors took tea together regularly; no doubt to discuss personal, as well as more abstruse philosophical matters. The atmosphere was relaxed and is captured for us many years later by Lucy Aikin writing to a friend, when she observes,[62]

> 'Long before my time, my kindred the Jennings, the Belshams, my excellent grandfather Aikin . . . had begun to break forth out of the chains and darkness of Calvinism, and their manners softened with their system. My youth was spent among the disciples or fellow-labourers of Price and Priestley, the descendants of Dr. John Taylor, the Arian, or in the society of that most amiable of men, Dr. Enfield. Amongst them was no rigorism. Dancing, cards, the theatre, were all held lawful in moderation.'

On another occasion writing to Henry Bright she says,[63]

> 'I have often thought with envy of that society. Neither Oxford nor Cambridge could boast of brighter names in literature or science than several of the Dissenting Tutors – humbly content, in an obscure town on a scanty pittance, to cultivate in themselves and communicate to a rising generation those mental acquirements and moral habits which are their own exceeding great reward. They and theirs lived together like one large family, and in the facility of their intercourse they found large compensation for its deficiency in luxury and splendour.'

Woodblock of Eyres Warrington Advertiser.

In the end the scanty pittance was not enough for Priestley and his growing family. It would be wrong to describe him as a restless soul, or to think him greedy. He was too well balanced and idealistic for that, but his many interests did draw him in different directions. As already noted, he was primarily a minister, and that vocation was always at the centre of his life. It took a secondary place while he was at the Academy, and again when he was with Lord Shelburne at Bowood and in London; but always he returned to it as his true vocation.

After Warrington he moved to Leeds, in what was one of his most active pastoral and spiritual phases, with a great burst of theological writing. But even then his other interests were not forgotten. Living next to a brewery he could not keep his nose out of the 'different kinds of air' which emerged.[64] Thus he encountered 'fixed air' (carbon dioxide); and so among his many bequests to humanity we must include soda water!

Chapter 5
THE TURN OF THE TIDE
(1770-1786)

'Now here, you see, it takes all the running you can do, to stay in the same place. If you want to get somewhere else, you must run at least twice as fast!'

'Through the Looking Glass', by Lewis Carroll.

The active life of Warrington Academy was twenty-six years. In retrospect it can be seen that its fortune changed drastically at the halfway stage, although there were still many fruitful years ahead, and just as many students still to come. Following Priestley's departure, the high standard which he had set was never reached again, but the event which was to have the greatest impact on the establishment was the untimely **death of John Seddon** in January 1770. Turner,[1] who was a student at the Academy in the late 1770s, attributes his death to 'a violent fever'; McLachlan says[2] he 'died from a seizure whilst on horseback'. Whatever the cause the Academy had lost the mainspring of its activity and would never recover from the blow. He was not yet forty-five years old, and many years of devoted service might still have been expected of him. The Academy, with his ministry, was the whole of his life and he asked for nothing more.

In 1772 John Holt died, so the three who had staffed the Academy in its first year were all dead. The link remaining between the early and the later period was John Aikin. He was not directly responsible for management or discipline, but there is no doubt that, in spite of the many difficulties through which the institution was to pass in the years remaining, his benign temperament had a steadying influence right up to his death in 1780.

Schools in Warrington today employ German and French assistants to aid the teaching in their language departments. These are young teachers who are native speakers, and as such they give great encouragement to the pupils, supplementing the work of permanent staff. Two centuries earlier Warrington Academy was already employing the same technique, though not in quite the

WA—F

same way. Gone were the days of Jennings' Academy at Kibworth, when French was taught without any knowledge of pronunciation.

The first appointment of this kind came after Priestley's departure, when **John Reinhold Forster**[3] was appointed to teach Modern Languages and Natural History. He was a German from Danzig, educated at the Royal College of Berlin and the University of Halle. He spoke German and French fluently. He was an expert on Mineralogy, on which he published a 'Syllabus of Lectures' while at Warrington. He was also considered one of the best botanists of the day, collaborating with Anna Blackburne at Orford Hall, where he was a regular visitor. It was arranged that he should lecture in alternate years on Mineralogy and Botany. Also, as the Academy catered for young men destined for the Army and Navy, he offered a course of lectures on 'Fortification, Gunnery, and Tactics, if a sufficient number of young gentlemen should desire it.'

In spite of its promise this was not a successful appointment. Henry Bright tells us,[4] 'Mr. Forster, . . . remained at Warrington but a short time; his irritable temper, and the entire want of economy which he displayed in all his arrangements, made him out of place in a situation where mutual forbearance and courtesy were so much required, and where, among the tutors at least, extravagance was unknown.' Two young Forsters were students at the Academy at this time, George and Charles. It appears that they were not popular with their fellow students.[5] William Hare, writing home to his father in Cork in 1769, 'complained that Forster's children spied on the students and reported every idle tale.'

It seems the trustees were forced to terminate Forster's engagement and McLachlan tells us[6] that, 'His Prussian manners and discipline may have evoked the resolution of the trustees in 1769 desiring the students to appoint a committee to air their grievances year by year.'

Around this time Reinhold Forster had an LL.D. degree conferred on him by Oxford University, and then joined Captain Cook's second voyage, accompanied by his son George. It is interesting to note that Priestley had already been considered for the position and turned down. He himself comments,[7] 'Mr Banks informed me that I was objected to by some clergymen in the Board of Longitude, who had direction of this business, on account of my religious principles; and presently after I heard that Dr. Forster, a person far better qualified for the purpose, had got the appointment.'

Was Forster really so much better qualified? It seems doubtful, but it is an example of Priestley's characteristic humility and deference. It is also an example of the extraordinary power which the Anglican establishment could exercise to block an appointment which was not in the religious field. On returning to Europe Forster became a Professor at the University of Halle.

William Turner reports[8] that after Forster the trustees employed a succession of French teachers, a Monsieur Fantin la Tour, a Monsieur le Maitre or Mara, and Lewis Guery. 'At length, the trustees resolved to engage **Mr. Hulme**, an English gentleman who had resided abroad, who continued to teach French, and also fencing, to such as chose it, till the close of the academy.'

It is asserted that Monsieur le Maitre, alias Mara, was none other than the notorious French revolutionary, **Jean Paul Marat**. McLachlan reviews[9] the evidence at some length, but as there is no reference to be found in the minute book or the Trustees Annual Reports (those for 1771 and 1772 are missing) he concludes that the case is 'not proven'. However G.A. Carter,[10] in his introduction to Turner's text, points out that previous writers 'have overlooked the Academy accounts which are contained in the same volume as the Register of Admissions at Manchester College, Oxford.' Here there is an entry dated September 1771 for £3.3s to 'Mr. Mara for journey' followed by French Master's fees and journey (presumably the return journey) in June 1772, and incidentally Mara was how he spelt his name at that time.

The most significant appointment after Seddon's demise was that of the **Rev. William Enfield**;[11] in fact he filled all of Seddon's posts. There was an agreement between the Sankey Street Chapel congregation and the Academy Trustees to have one man, and so Enfield became minister, tutor in 'Belles Lettres', Secretary to the Trustees, and Rector of the Academy. He was born in Suffolk and educated at Daventry, after which he went to Liverpool as pastor at Benn's Garden, from whence he came to Warrington.

Enfield appears to have been a charming man and tireless worker. Mounfield describes him as 'an amiable and diligent man, eloquent and persuasive in the pulpit, and delightful in society'. Yet, he failed in the qualities that the Academy most needed . . . 'It was mastership, not scholarship that was the need of the hour.' His colleague, friend, admirer and first biographer, the younger John Aikin, gives a similar assessment.[12] He says, 'Whatever could be effected by those amiable endowments which conciliate affection, might be hoped from one who was to become the delight of a large circle of acquaintance; but in those emergencies where firmness, resolution, and a kind of dignified severity of conduct might be requisite, there was cause to apprehend a failure.' This is not damning with faint praise, it is merely acknowledging a vital flaw in one who should never have been burdened with the task of pupil management, on top of everything else.

There is no doubt as to Enfield's scholarship and his success as a tutor. His great strength was in English Literature and Elocution;

William Turner praises 'the purity of his style, and the general elegance of his turn of thought'. His anthology of prose and verse 'The Speaker', with introductory essays 'On Elocution' and 'On Reading Works of Taste', was first printed at Eyres' Press in 1774.[13] It reached its fourth edition while the Academy was in operation, then two more in his own lifetime. An eighth edition in 1801 was the last printed by Eyres', but many later editions appeared as far afield as London, Dublin, Paris and Boston. The last edition in the British Museum catalogue was issued in 1858, eighty-four years after the first. His other publications included 'Prayers for Families', a 'Preachers Directory' and a 'History of Liverpool'.

He was honoured by Edinburgh University with a doctorate (LL.D.) in 1774. Again, as in the case of Priestley, the initiative came from Thomas Percival, who by then was an established physician in Manchester and a trustee of the Academy. In acceding to this request Principal Robertson wrote to Percival,

> 'We wish in this College not to confer honorary degrees, either in Divinity or Law, without duly considering the merit of the candidates. But I am happy when we can confer that mark of esteem on any of our Dissenting Brethren. Mr. Enfield appears to me a very ingenuous and deserving man.'

In addition to Language and Literature Enfield was also tutor in History, Geography and Commerce; and after a few years he had to take on Mathematics as well.[14] He lived in the house previously occupied by the Priestleys, but he took his meals and presided at table in the students' refectory. Students at the Academy came from far and wide throughout Britain, Ireland and the Colonies. Colonials appear in the list from the second year onwards, but there is a cluster in the years around 1770 when Enfield took over as Rector, and these appear to have been particularly troublesome; a bad influence on the community as a whole.

William Turner, who entered the Academy in 1777 gives a vivid account of Enfield's problems:[15]

> '. . . though, amidst the heterogeneous mass of students in this seminary, he generally engaged the esteem and warm affection of the orderly and sober part, he was not always treated with due respect by those, even among these classes, who had no particular interest in the credit and success of the institution; while by the dissipated and inflamed West Indian, whose pastime it had been from his youth to sport with human sufferings – by the profligate outcast of our great public schools, who had learned all the evil, without any of the good, of those estab-

lishments, and was sent hither as a sort of *dernier resort* – and by the pampered petling of fortune who, from the treatment he had seen given, and been allowed to give, to his private tutor at home, had learned to consider every tutor as a sort of upper servant, – he was sometimes treated with a degree of scornful insolence, which nothing but a forbearance like his could tolerate, and which it required the occasional co-operation of the other tutors effectually to check.'

Turner goes on to mention one of his own contemporaries who used to boast that 'the first request of the children of planters to their parents was for a young neger to kick'. There is here an implied and damning indictment of the Academy's management in the later years. Turner concludes this part of his report thus,

'He (Enfield) made several attempts to deliver him from this burden, and after the failure of repeated attempts to obtain a successor in this department, he addressed a strong remonstrance to the Trustees, which put an end to the institution.'

It also seems from this account that the continued stress had a deleterious effect on the Rector's own health, resulting almost certainly in a peptic ulcer. After the Academy ceased to function he continued his ministry, and with this he combined private tuition for a few students during his remaining years at Warrington. Thus it might appear that the academic wheel had come full circle, since the minister at Sankey Street Chapel in 1784-85 could be said to be conducting a small, private, single tutor academy, as in the case of Charles Owen when he started in 1696. But after just two years he moved to Norwich, where he lived the remainder of his life.

Other Tutors in the Later Years.

In spite of the difficulties outlined, teaching at the Academy did not immediately deteriorate after 1770. Aikin and Enfield formed the stable element, just as Aikin, Holt and Priestley had done in earlier years. As the Academy catered for men destined for Trade, Commerce and Politics, as well as the more philosophical, Business Studies were not neglected. A local man, **Jacob Bright**,[16] was employed for two hours a day for over twenty years to teach writing, shorthand, drawing, book-keeping and surveying. He was paid £20 per annum with the addition of fees paid by the students who took these courses; one guinea for the writing and book-keeping and two guineas for the surveying. It is to be hoped that his other hours in the week were more lucrative.

John Aikin (junior)[17] when he completed his studies at the Academy went as an apprentice to an apothecary at Uppingham in Rutland. Then, at the age of eighteen, he moved to Edinburgh to study medicine under the tuition of some of the most remarkable teachers of the day – Black, Munro and Cullen. Next he moved to Manchester, to be what we would now term a post-graduate student, under Charles White, F.R.S.,[18] a leading surgeon and obstetrician, who was one of the founders of the Infirmary there. White was an original and provocative thinker and teacher, from whom Aikin learned much. At the same time he enjoyed the stimulating company of his former fellow-student at the Academy, Thomas Percival, by then established in practice in Manchester. In

John Aikin M.D. (1747-1822)

the winter of 1769 he travelled to London to join the class of the great anatomist Dr. William Hunter. He lodged with his uncle Jennings in Bloomsbury, where he fell in love with his cousin Martha; thus, when they were married, adding another link to the Kibworth association. But first he moved to Chester where he hoped to establish himself in practice. He did not meet with success, but established a firm and lifelong friendship with Dr. John Haygarth, one of the pioneers of small-pox prevention, and the treatment of infectious fevers. In succeeding years they used to meet regularly at a hostelry in Frodsham, to share a meal and discuss matters of mutual interest.

Following this short interlude Aikin moved back to Warrington, where he established himself in practice as a physician. His arrival followed shortly upon the appointment of Enfield to head the Academy, and he himself joined the staff as a part-time tutor, in which capacity he remained until the establishment collapsed in 1783, when he left the town for good. He was not paid by the Academy, receiving only the direct fees of students. He was engaged mainly for the benefit of those going on to study Medicine and, as Fulton[19] remarked, these 'had been admirably prepared in the Academy'. He gave courses in alternate years on Anatomy and Physics in the first year, and Chemistry in the second. In his time Priestley had given some lectures on Anatomy, but was a student in Chemistry.

The first issue of the 'Medical Register'[20] devotes two pages to Warrington Academy. In this the statement occurs: 'Mr Aikin proposes to give to any Gentlemen who are designed for the Medical profession a Course of private Instructions preparatory to the regular study of Physic'. Later it adds that 'Many Gentlemen of the Medical Profession have passed through a complete course of Academical Learning at Warrington previous to their commencing the study of Physic at the University'. Of these it lists seven of the better known, not including Aikin himself.

It is interesting that this report refers to Aikin as a surgeon. This exceeds the title of apothecary, but denies him the distinction of physician which he later attained after he had left the Academy, when he travelled to Leiden and took his M.D.. Even then he was denied the ultimate cachet – Fellowship of the Royal College of Physicians, as his doctorate was not from Oxbridge.

Aikin owed his inspiration to Priestley, whose earlier efforts in the same direction added a further dimension to his remarkable achievements as a tutor at the Academy.

Like other tutors, the younger Aikin availed himself of Eyres' Press to publish a number of works. For the use of his students he brought out a 'Sketch of Animal Anatomy' and 'Heads of Chemistry'. He had previously published his 'Thoughts on Hospitals'

(1771).[21] This is a most significant contribution to hygiene in hospital practice, the standard of which in many instances at the time, and even well into the nineteenth century, was quite deplorable. Aikin and his colleague Percival (in an addendum) advocate such simple measures as cleanliness, fresh air, space between beds, and the proper disposal of contaminated clothing and dressings: ideas which are so basic that we are apt today to undervalue the contribution of these pioneers.

Fulton comments[22] on Aikin's book that it displays 'signs of originality and independence throughout which seem not to have been referred to by the historians of English medicine'. He goes on to explain 'the belief that wound infection is due to a viable agent transmitted by the air, or by direct contact' as not being entirely new, and gives particular credit to Charles White of Manchester, who trained Aikin, Percival and others. But he adds, 'The ideas were *actively applied* and this . . . is the greatest single advance in medicine that was made by the Warrington group'. (It would have been more accurate to refer to the Manchester-Warrington group.) In 1773 Aikin produced the first 'Bill of Mortality' for the town of Warrington with a short commentary, which established a pattern to be followed in the years ahead. In this he was reflecting the pioneering work and the inspiration of his friend Thomas Percival in Manchester.

Another significant work written by Aikin, and published at the end of this period, was his 'Biographical Memoirs of Medicine in Great Britain' (1780), which deals with the period 'From the Revival of Literature to the time of Harvey' (thirteenth to sixteenth century). He also published other scientific works, with books on Classical Literature and Natural History. He wrote 'A Description of the Country from thirty to forty miles around Manchester' which, of course, included Warrington. He published 'Essays on Song Writing with a Collection of English Songs'.

Another task which engaged him in those days was assisting **John Howard** with the publication of his monumental work on **'The State of the Prisons'**.[23] Howard was a meticulous and tireless observer and recorder, whose great work was unsurpassed, but he was no literary genius. John Aikin induced him to come to Warrington to have the book printed at Eyres' Press, while he acted as editor, thus ensuring a work that was not only informative, but readable as well.

Aikin collaborated with his sister Anna Laetitia to produce a book of essays[24] on general topics which was highly commended, and a book for children entitled **'Evenings at Home'**[25] which was so popular that it went through numerous editions until well on into the nineteenth century. It might be described as an insight into how a cultured middle class English family entertained itself before the advent of gramophone, radio, cinema and television.

It was not until 1784, after he had left Warrington, that Aikin went to Leiden to obtain his M.D., for which he submitted a thesis on 'Milk Secretion in the Puerperium'. His memoirs contain[26] a fascinating day by day account of this excursion. Thereafter he settled for a time in Yarmouth and then in London, until failing health forced him to retire. In 1798 he moved to Stoke Newington near the home of his sister, where he lived out his life until 1822. Both he and Anna Laetitia are buried in the same family tomb in the graveyard of the old parish church there.

Even in retirement he set aside an hour every morning to provide medical advice for poorer neighbours, but that was the limit of his medical practice for the remaining years. However, his literary output was still prodigious. His major work at this time was the **'General Biography'** in ten volumes which Fulton refers to as 'a predecessor of the Dictionary of National Biography'. This was started in collaboration with William Enfield, but this friend died in 1797 when the work was only a year in progress, and working on his own Aikin did not reach volume ten until 1815. He went on to write 'Annals of the Reign of King George III' in two volumes, covering the whole reign.

With his earlier work on medical biography John Aikin had found the libraries he consulted most unco-operative; the bias against Dissenters conditioned their response. But in London he found the library of the Royal College of Physicians contained much that he required. He started to work there, but in only a short time he was barred from further access because he was not a Fellow of the College. He and other licentiates complained that they could not become Fellows, whatever their merits or higher qualifications, unless they had an Oxbridge degree; but Dissenters they remained, and so the access remained barred.[27]

Like many of his friends Aikin did not hesitate to express his opinions in public, as well as in private, and these were not calculated to endear them to those in power. In 1786, writing to his friend Dr. John Haygarth in Chester, who, as an Anglican and an Oxford graduate, was closer to the establishment and thus did not always share his views, he comments on the Dutch whom he had observed at close quarters during his trip to Leiden, saying, 'Why need a republic tie themselves to the control of hereditary fools.'[28] Later he published an article in the 'Gentleman's Magazine' on **'The Rights of the Poor'**,[29] which had much in common with Tom Paine's 'Rights of Man'. He was involved, as also was his sister, with the movement for the Repeal of the Test Acts. But like so many of the liberal dissenters it was his sympathy with the early aspirations of the French Revolution which really damned him in the eyes of the establishment.

Lucy Aikin tells us how her father was treated at that time by members of the community which he had hitherto served,[30]

> 'Of the clergy resident in and near Yarmouth,... one alone had the courage and liberality to stand by him . . . The members of the corporation and the high party generally . . . were pleased to consider themselves absolved by circumstances, from the engagement to support him, into which they had voluntarily entered on his coming to Yarmouth, . . . they entered into secret machinations for inviting another physician to take up his abode among them.'

She also tells of her own sufferings at that time,[31]

Lucy Aikin (1781-1846) author, family archivist and recorder.

'I should scarcely be believed were I to recount the bitter persecution we poor children underwent in the children's parties we frequented . . . What was the lot of us poor little ones? Children persecuted by children for words, for names, of the meaning of which none of them had the slightest conception. I have sat a whole evening while others were dancing, because nobody would dance with a Presbyterian. I have been pushed, hunted, even struck, as I stood silent and helpless to the cry of Presbyterian.'

Many years later, reflecting on this psychological trauma and the ways in which it affected her own personality, and writing to her friend Dr. Ellery Channing in America she declared,[32]

'The atmosphere of a sect and a party, which it was my fate to breathe from childhood, narrowed my affections within strait limits. Under the notion of a generous zeal for freedom, truth, and virtue, I cherished a set of prejudices and antipathies which placed beyond the pale of my charity not the few, but the many, the mass of my compatriots. I shudder now to think *how good a hater* I was in the days of my youth. Time and reflection and a wider range of acquaintance, and a calmer state of the public mind, mitigated by degrees my bigotry; but I really knew not what it was to open my heart to the human race until I had drunk deeply into the spirit of your writings.'

The individual is indeed fortunate who can have such clear insight, and who, furthermore, can pass on these reflections for the benefit of others. Prejudice, antipathies and bigotry are not dead, nor ever will be, and we must be grateful for the sobering influence of a generous commentator.

Persecution of dissenters had been dying out after the mid-century when Warrington Academy was founded; but now with the American Revolt and the French Revolution it was resurrected. The experience of John Aikin and his family is a good example of what was to be expected by any who shared their views.

Before leaving the Aikin family it is appropriate to reflect again on its cohesive influence on the society of Warrington Academy; the original children had grown up; young John had moved away to pursue his career; his sister had remained and was very much involved in the social life of students, staff and associates. Then John returned as a fully fledged medical man; and soon after Anna Laetitia married Mr. Barbauld, leaving Warrington for good at that time.

The next generation began to appear, and there is much in their later writings and correspondence to tell of life in Warrington. But it is John's daughter, Lucy, more than any other, who gives us so many insights into life at the Academy in its later years, as well as the progress of the family thereafter. Had the institution continued to flourish and her father remained on the staff she might well have assumed the mantle of her aunt Laetitia as time progressed.

As the Academy moved into its final phase the trustees remained hopeful in spite of all difficulties, and continued to make significant staff appointments up until the end. After Holt's death in 1772 they appointed the **Rev. George Walker,**[33] who, like Seddon, was a graduate of Kendal Academy, to be Mathematics' Tutor. However being newly married he was not able to subsist on the poor stipend he received, and so after only two years he accepted an invitation from Nottingham and departed.

Pendlebury Houghton[34] entered the Academy as a Divinity student in 1773, and on the completion of his five year course was invited to remain as assistant to the elderly and ailing John Aikin (senior). But after only a year the old man was dead, and with the prospect of a new full time appointment, there was no place for this young, inexperienced graduate, although in the circumstances of fifty years earlier he might well have become a successor. It is interesting to note that his father had been a student in Doddridge's Academy. Pendlebury Houghton moved to Manchester as minister at Dob Lane, then to Shrewsbury and later to Norwich where he was assistant and eventually successor to Dr. Enfield.

In the year leading up to Aikin's death the trustees looked around for a Classics tutor to relieve him. They settled upon **Gilbert Wakefield, B.A.;**[35] and the fact that the management was still sanguine is borne out in a letter from Sir Henry Hoghton, M.P., the Academy's President, which expresses a hope on behalf of the trustees, 'that your connection with this seminary will be as agreeable to you, as it will be respectable to them.' Turner, who had come to the Academy in 1777, became one of Wakefield's pupils, and has left a glowing account of his virtues as a tutor, and an inspiration to youth. He was engaged to teach Modern Literature as well as Classics.

Gilbert Wakefield was a Classics graduate of Cambridge, Second Wrangler in 1776, and a Fellow of Jesus College. He came to Liverpool as an Anglican curate, but turned to Arianism and resigned from office. Nevertheless, a letter from Theophilus Lindsey (who himself followed the same path) to Turner in 1783 reveals that 'he uniformly attended the worship of the Church of England at Warrington', rather than Enfield's chapel. Lindsey continues, 'I hope time will mellow his disposition and lessen the high opinion he seems to have of himself'. Wakefield was recommended by Priestley and by Dr. John Jebb who had been his tutor at Cambridge, (another man who left the Church of England at that time to become an Arian).

There is no doubt of Wakefield's ability, nor of his service to the Academy while it lasted; but a note of arrogance keeps breaking through, with an eccentricity of behaviour. After the Academy's demise he taught for a time at the newly established Hackney College. Then he fell foul of the law, when he was indicted for the terrible crime of 'Seditious Libel'. This unspeakable offence is one that is indulged in with impunity in our own time, almost every day, by politicians, journalists and citizens at large. It is the terrible crime of criticising the establishment, secular and clerical!

We may consider the matter amusing now, but it was no joke for Gilbert Wakefield, John Wilkes, Tom Paine, Hamilton Rowan and many others at that time. Wakefield was foolish enough to take on the Bishop of Llandaff. He was tried, found guilty and imprisoned. Gaol is bad enough at any time, but a quick perusal of John Howard's book soon conveys how much worse it was then, with the everpresent hazard of gaol fever in addition to all the other evils. Wakefield survived the ordeal, but not for long, as his health was irreparably damaged.

Donald Davie in his Clark Lectures (1976)[36] on the theme of 'A Gathered Church', castigates Wakefield as 'an unmanageable coxcomb' and cites the correspondence, in verse, between himself and Aikin, on his release from prison, where he refers to 'That first of comforts to the soul, the plaudit of a conscience self-approv'd;' and in a later line, 'Self in benevolence absorb'd and lost.' Is this fair? Others who have survived a living martyrdom in similar circumstances have expressed much the same sentiments, though perhaps in more self-effacing terms, and been applauded. However, irrespective of any final judgement on his character, Gilbert Wakefield served Warrington Academy well. The terraced house in Bewsey Street in which he lived still stands, has been refurbished in recent years, and is marked with a plaque.

With the death of Dr. Aikin (senior) came the very last appointment to the Academy's staff. The man chosen for Divinity tutor was **Rev. Nicholas Clayton**,[37] then at Benn's Garden, Liverpool, where Enfield had been before him. Clayton was a former student of Northampton and Daventry, where he had been a contemporary of Priestley; and then of Glasgow University where he was with George Walker. On coming to Warrington he gave lectures on Logic, Metaphysics and Morals, with overall responsibility for Divinity. However in this faculty there remained but one student. To mark his appointment the University of Edinburgh conferred on him the degree of D.D.; Principal Robertson acceding to the recommendation of Thomas Butterworth Bayley, an old Edinburgh student, and Vice-President of the Academy. The Academy paid the fee for the diploma, probably because the trustees felt badly about Clayton's appointment now that the decline was so obvious; and indeed shortly afterwards teaching was suspended. In September 1783 Benjamin Vaughan, writing to Samuel Heywood from London, mentions that Clayton had visited him. 'I think it my duty,' he states, 'to tell you that Dr. Clayton has been very ill-used.' Eventually he was voted a sum of one hundred guineas 'as a consideration of the peculiar circumstances attending his case as late tutor.'

Clayton, like Priestley, was something of a polymath, being particularly skilled in Mathematics and Science. Some years earlier he had assisted when Walker left and Enfield was forced to undertake the teaching of Mathematics. Enfield applied himself, taking a crash course during his vacation under Clayton's tuition, after which he attained a reasonable proficiency in the subject. Turner reports of Clayton that[38]

> 'He was not merely a theoretical but a practical mechanic; he was an excellent workman, both with the lathe and in cabinet work. Some of the most accurate and highly finished articles in the Warrington apparatus were invented and finished by him during his residence at Liverpool, for the use of his friend Dr. Enfield. An apparatus for demonstrating the laws of the composition and resolution of forces, another for the phenomena of the collision of elastic and non-elastic bodies, and a pair of whirling tables, the comparative velocities of each of which might be accurately adjusted according to a variety of rates, are recollected as particularly curious.'

With Clayton's appointment the Academy was fully staffed again, and, on paper at least, was as well served as at any time during its existence. Enfield and Wakefield were the other full time tutors, with part-time service from John Aikin (junior), lecturing on Chemistry and Anatomy, Hulme on French and Bright for Business Studies. But McLachlan comments,[39]

> 'From the date of Aikin's death, though not then foreseen, the ultimate fate of the Academy was sealed. As a tutor since its foundation no man had done more for the Academy, and none had enjoyed such universal respect and esteem from students, colleagues, and supporters of the institution. "His influence over the students," says one of them, "was very great, and arose not merely from the excellence of his instruction, but from the kind concern which he took in their welfare." In the circumstances then prevailing the loss was irreparable. A few generous

> friends had relieved the urgency of the financial situation by substantial donations, but there was no endowment for any "chair". Students' fees had declined with their numbers, whilst the "scare" of Marat's supposed connection with the Academy and the wild exploits of some of its pupils had reduced or eliminated the subscriptions of timid subscribers. Yet hope still prevailed among enthusiasts, and the work went on – for a time.'

Between the suspension of teaching in 1783, and the final decision to close the Academy for good in 1786, a few more desperate attempts were made to breathe fresh life into the corpse. In July 1783 there was a proposal to unite Warrington Academy with Daventry, under Thomas Belsham, a cousin of the Aikins, but this failed because the Daventry trustees could not accept the terms suggested for the merger. In June 1785 Belsham was approached again with a request that he should leave Daventry and take over direction of the Academy at Warrington. He wavered for a time but finally decided against accepting, and thus the fate of the establishment at Warrington was finally sealed.

Chapter 6
STUDENTS AND SOCIAL LIFE AT WARRINGTON ACADEMY

'Why was it that many of the most important contributions to English Medicine and Science in the eighteenth century came from a rather restricted geographical district in and about the County of Lancashire? During this period the English Universities contributed almost nothing. The Royal Society in London attracted a few men, but major contributions from the district of London were significantly few. Edinburgh had more to offer, but quite suddenly in Lancashire one finds a group of men making substantial contributions to medicine, science, literature and art.'

J.F.Fulton, M.D.(1933)[1]

In the twenty-six years that the Warrington Academy was active, about four hundred students passed through;[2] an average just above fifteen per year. For Divinity students the course was five years, and for all others three years; so that, allowing for the lean years at the beginning and end, for most of the time there would have been about fifty in residence.

This Academy has been referred to, disparagingly at times, as a Unitarian Seminary, but the facts belie any such label. Like all the other academies, a primary aim was to prepare young men for the ministry, but most of them catered also for the other learned professions. Warrington broadened these aims to include men destined for civil and active life in Trade, Industry, Commerce and Politics.

The *Divinity students* over the years amounted to fifty-five in all, of whom fifteen went into the Church of England. Nathaniel Alexander of Derry was Bishop successively of Clonfert, Down and Connor, and finally Meath. William Cookson, D.D. became a Canon of Windsor. William Bruce, D.D. was Principal of Belfast Academy. Thomas Barnes, D.D. and Ralph Harrison, ministers at Cross Street Chapel, were to be the principal Divinity tutors at the successor Academy to Warrington in Manchester. William Howell

WA—G

became a tutor at Carmarthen Academy. William Turner settled in Newcastle-upon-Tyne, had a long association with Manchester Academy and Manchester College, York, and was the first historian of his Alma Mater. Rev. James Allen came from Ireland as a private tutor to John Jacob, to whose father he was private chaplain. He availed himself of the opportunity to attend Dr. Aikin's lectures and so was enrolled as a pupil. Dr. Benjamin Dawson, divine and philologist, was another private tutor who came to Warrington with Sir James Ibbetson, a young baronet from Leeds, and joined the literary coterie there.

So, with less than 14% of the students taking Divinity the Academy could hardly be called a seminary, and with just over 27% of

Rev. Wm. Turner of Newcastle-upon-Tyne. Graduate of Warrington Academy and its first historian. This portrait is from around the time when he wrote his articles in the Monthly Repository (1813-15).

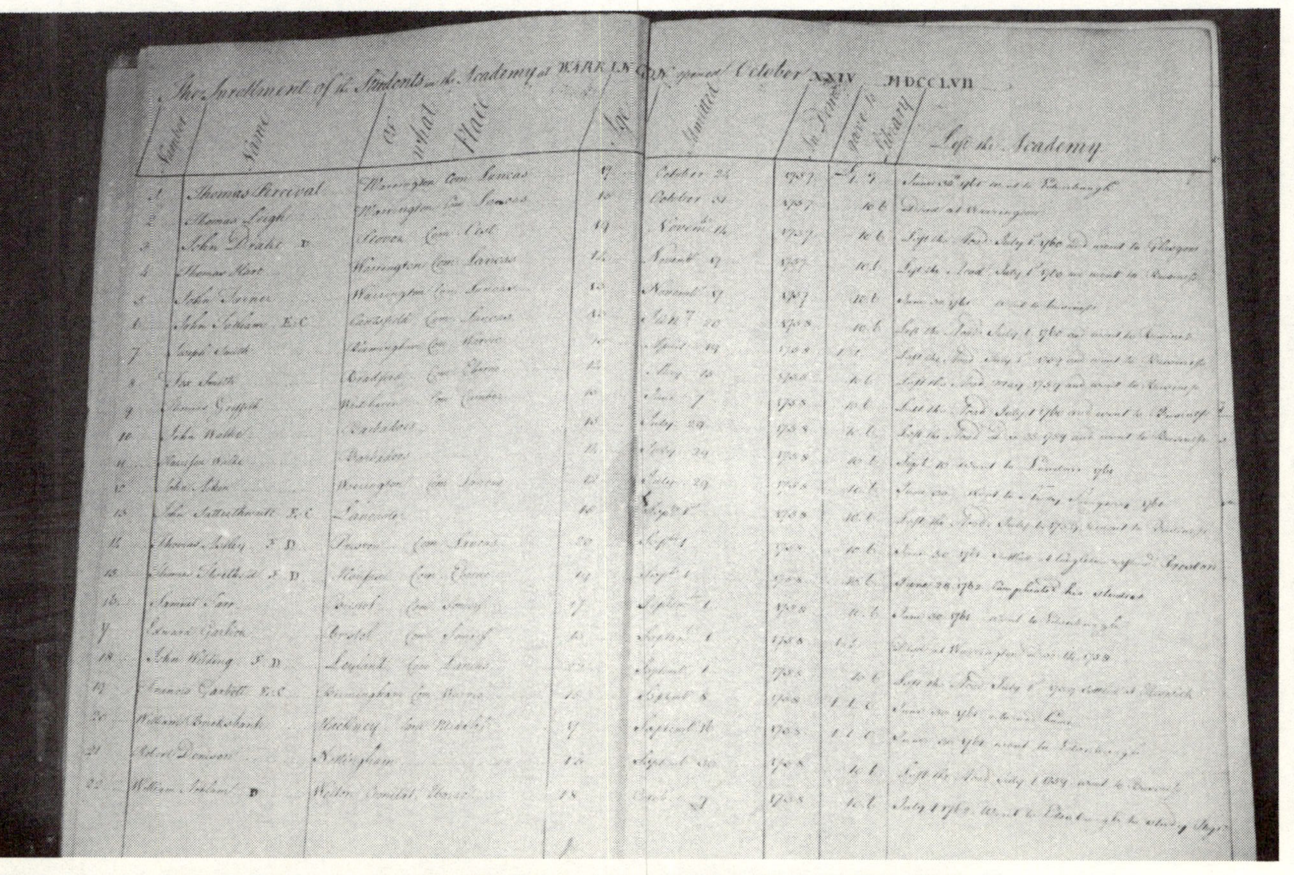

Warrington Academy Roll – first page (1757-1758) from library of Manchester College Oxford.

those going into the Church of England, whatever leanings the tutors might have, it could hardly be designated a Unitarian establishment. The label more properly fits this Academy's successors. The fact is that evolution was occurring, but had not yet run its full course.

Law claimed twenty-four students. Samuel Heywood, who went on to Cambridge, eventually became Chief Justice of Wales. Isaac Baugh became Secretary to the Supreme court at Calcutta. Samuel Benyon was Attorney General for the County of Chester, and James Clerk became Sheriff of Edinburgh. Amongst others, Charles J. Harford was a close friend of Edmund Burke. Edmund Calamy was grandson of the ejected minister with the same name, who had been historian to that generation, and John Doddridge Humphreys was grandson of Philip Doddridge of Northampton.

Medicine had twenty-one students, of whom *Thomas Percival*,[3] as already mentioned, was the Academy's first student and most distinguished. He was a Warrington youth who had his early education at the Boteler Grammar School. He was also the third generation of his family to practise medicine in the town. However he soon moved to Manchester where, during a distinguished career, he was a pioneer in public and occupational health, as well as a distinguished writer on medical ethics.[4] It is claimed by American authors that his book on the subject was the model for the code of ethics of the American Medical Association.[5] He was a Trustee of Warrington Academy and later of Manchester Academy, of which he became President. He was also a founder member of the Manchester Literary and Philosophical Society, and for many years its president.

John Aikin, a son of the Rev. John Aikin, entered

Thomas Percival M.D. (1740-1804).

the Academy in its second year at the early age of eleven. Like Percival and Samuel Farr, another contemporary, he went on to Edinburgh for his medical training and eventually took his M.D. at Leiden. His distinguished career has already been sketched in the last chapter. Edward Rigby, grandson of the Rev. Dr. John Taylor, and brother of the notorious Misses Sally and Lizzie, became a distinguished practitioner at Norwich, as also did Philip Meadows Martineau of the well known dissenter family in that city. Caleb Hillier Parry settled at Bath, where he achieved fame as an agriculturalist as well as a physician; he married Sally Rigby.

The influence of Joseph Priestley, who introduced the subjects of Chemistry and Anatomy to the Academy's curriculum, to be carried on later by John Aikin after he had qualified, was an important stimulus to those young men who eventually decided on Medicine as a career. Their favourite Medical School was Edinburgh, which at that time in the great days of Cullen, Munro and Black, was ousting Leiden as Europe's leading school, but many still went to Leiden for their doctorate.

In *Politics* Benjamin Vaughan, M.P. and Francis Garbett were involved in Lord Shelburne's administration, which negotiated with France and made peace with the American Colonies. Henry Beaufoy was M.P. for Calne in Wiltshire (again a connection with Shelburne) and twice promoted bills for repeal of the Test Acts, but without success. **Henry Laurens** from Charleston, South Carolina, was son of the President of Congress during the War of Independence.

Archibald Hamilton Rowan,[6] born in London of Irish parents, was educated at Westminster School and Cambridge, from whence he was rusticated and recommended by his tutor Dr.John Jebb to Warrington Academy. In later years he settled in Ireland, was a leader of the Volunteers, and later of the United Irishmen, was indicted on a charge of 'seditious libel' and was committed to gaol for two years. In the early months of his imprisonment he was involved in negotiations between an emissary of France and the United Irish leader Wolfe Tone, which left him liable to a charge of high treason and almost certain to be hanged. However he made a dramatic escape from gaol, going first to France, where he did not relish living through the Reign of Terror, and soon moving on to America. Whilst he was in Paris he was visited by Benjamin Vaughan. Mary Wolstonecraft was another refugee in that city at the time, while Tom Paine was in one of its gaols, and he was in contact with both. Rowan remained an exile in America till the turn of the century, thereby missing the Irish insurrection of 1798. He was eventually granted a royal pardon and allowed to return home to his family in Ireland, where he lived on to a ripe old age, suffering the classical fate of a surviving, unsuccessful revolutionary, almost total oblivion; and Warrington Academy escaped the doubtful distinction of having a graduate hanged for treason!

About one hundred former students went into *Commerce*, and the remainder are hard to classify. In many cases it is obvious that contact was lost, and some may well have swelled the numbers in the vocational groups already outlined. Many also have vague labels such as 'country gentleman', but this heterogeneous group contains some who were well known in their time, and some who are still remembered.

John Goodriche was deaf from an early age following a fever (perhaps measles), but learned to overcome his disability. He was an able mathematician and distinguished himself as an astronomer, winning the Royal Society's Copley Medal for an outstanding contribution in that field. George Forster, the son of John Reinhold Forster, left to accompany his father on Captain Cook's second voyage, in which he helped to record the findings. He later became Professor of Natural History at Cassel. Robert Malthus was an outstanding political economist, who is best remembered for his ideas on population control. John Wedgwood was the son of the great Josiah, who made a career in banking in the city. William Wilkinson, a younger brother of Mary Priestley, came to Warrington with her husband, Joseph, from his school in Nantwich. William later became an iron-master in his father's footsteps. Both the Wedgwood and the Wilkinson families afforded considerable support to Priestley in his scientific pursuits over the years.

Richard Anthony Markham, who changed his name to Salisbury, was a distinguished Botanist and member of the Linnaean Society. John Leland Maquay became a director of the Bank of Ireland, and Edward Corry was brother of the Irish Chancellor of the Exchequer. George Willoughby, Lord Parham, the seventeenth and last Baron, was grandson of Hugh, the fifteenth Baron, who was the Academy's first President, and whose unique notoriety came from the fact that he was the sole remaining representative of non-conformity in the Upper House.

Joseph Cookson, an army officer, was a devotee of the turf, whose chief claim to fame was ownership of a famous racehorse – Diamond. Others of note are Lord Ennismore; Sir James Carnegie; Samuel Farr, translator of Hippocrates; Samuel Galton, a Quaker philanthrophist and member of the Lunar Society, and a generous patron of Priestley; also Benjamin and Nathaniel Heywood, nephews of the Academy's Treasurer, who were partners in founding a Manchester bank which was known as Wm. Deacon's, became William & Glyn's, and is now absorbed in the Royal Bank of Scotland.

This list does not exhaust the field, but to extend it may exhaust the reader! The student body was a very mixed bunch, unlike what was found in many of the former academies. There were, of course, the single-minded and dedicated students as of yore, but McLachlan explains that the failure to attract more of these 'was due in part to the smaller constituency of radical dissenters and liberal churchmen'.[7] Financial stringency caused the trustees to aim at families of greater means, but this meant diluting the group of more serious students, with young men of a rather different temperament, who were indulged by their parents, and easily distracted from their studies.

Students were drawn from all over England, Scotland and Ireland, with a considerable number who came from, or had connections with, the West Indies, and a few from the American Colonies. The Caribbeans gave the greatest trouble as they were the least amenable to discipline. Warrington was able to indulge students in a variety of ways; the townsfolk welcomed additional trade, but complained bitterly when there were bad debts. Those who could afford it were able to keep a horse in nearby livery stables, and ride out when they chose. Angling and boating were readily to hand, and although guns were specifically forbidden exercise and legitimate sports were encouraged.

That there were more illicit pleasures to be had is underlined by the repeated publication in the trustees' annual reports of certain disciplinary strictures. There was to be no frequenting of taverns, nor any place of public diversion; nor were games of chance to be countenanced. Students were not to go out of town, nor to be absent all night, without leave from the tutors. Above all it was clearly stated that 'Students are strictly prohibited entering into intimacies with persons of mean or illiberal behaviour, and *especially those of immoral character*.' In 1773 the report added that, 'No student shall wear gold or silver lace on any part of his cloaths, laced ruffles, silk coat, waistcoat, or breeches, or fine silk stockings.'

A few years earlier in August 1768 Mr. Samuel Vaughan of Bristol[8] had written to John Seddon, the Rector, complaining of his two sons' excessive expenses and profligate habits. He says,

> '. . . the consequence of the expense is abundantly more pernicious, as it naturally leads to Levity, a love of pleasure, dissipation, and affectation of smartness; diverts the attention, and prevents the necessary application to serious thought and Study. When I sent my Sons to so great a distance, it was with a view to preserving them from the reigning contagion of a dissipated age, to imbibe good Morals, acquire knowledge, and to obtain a manly and solid way of thinking and acting, but they are returned

with high Ideas of modern refinements, of dress and external accomplishments, which, if ever necessary, yet resumed by them much too soon. As one instance – they think it a Sight to appear without having their hair Frissened, and this must be done by a dresser, even upon the Sabbath. No person can more wish for, and encourage an open and liberal way of thinking and acting than myself, yet do I think that day should be kept with Ancient Solemnity, for to say the least, the reverse gives offence to many serious good people, and exhibits an Ill example at a time when Religion is at so low an ebb . . . therefore any relaxation or Innovation under sanction of such a seminary as yours, may have the most pernicious tendency, for when restraints, even in unessentials, are removed they are frequently a clue to gradation, to the fashionable levity of the Age and Irreligion.'

Seddon had a further letter from the older son, Benjamin Vaughan, who stood thus indicted, expressing contrition for past excesses and promising reform. He is afraid his conduct may have reflected badly on the Academy, but believes that

'Ill natured people will say ill-natured things. They say we are gay and idle, business gives way to pleasure, and instead of receiving improvement we are taught how to live idly. This has been said in my hearing. But tho' I am certain that none of us has been viscious, but only gay, this has been laid to our charge. Our recreations have been innocent tho' expensive – but they imagine that they cannot be expensive without being criminal. I believe that none of us has received any injury from ye Liberty allowed us, but others may make a bad use of it.'

Later in their correspondence[9] he goes on to reveal his preoccupation with Politics, even at that early stage, assuring Seddon that the indomitable radical John Wilkes will probably get a pardon from the Crown and that he himself does not believe Wilkes ever wrote the infamous 'North Briton – No.45' (which of course he did). In the following February 1769 young Vaughan is writing again to Seddon to inform him of Wilkes' re-election to Parliament, and a week later he is sending him his hero's latest address in the hope that it might be placed in some coffee houses 'frequented by the better sort of People', and especially requesting that a copy be sent to Manchester.

The political fervour of students was just one of the phenomena that could make problems for the tutors from time to time, especially vis-à-vis the townspeople who might not share their enthusiasm. Bright tells us that[10]

> '. . . the politics of the students were no less inconvenient than their flirtations. Strong Whigs, and something more, as the tutors themselves were, they were alarmed and terrified at the anti-English zeal, which, during the American War, was displayed by several of the students. One of them, who boarded at Dr. Enfield's, insisted on his right to illuminate *his own* windows for an American victory; but this the Doctor refused to allow, as it committed himself, the master of the house.'

But higher pursuits were not entirely neglected in the leisure hours as Lucy Aikin relates:[11] 'The most cordial intimacy subsisted among the tutors and their families, with whom the elder students associated on terms of easy and affectionate intercourse; and while the various branches of human knowledge occupied their graver hours, the moments of recreation were animated by sports of wit and ingenuity well adapted to nerve the wing of youthful genius'.

It is vital in reviewing some of this literature to be mindful of the extent to which language usage has evolved, or else the innocent reader might begin to suspect unspeakable behaviour, much more serious than the evils which were forbidden by the trustees in their annual reports.

To **Anna Laetitia Aikin** more than any other we are indebted for a lively picture of the social life at the Academy. She is a true Warrington chauvinist, in the best sense. Her account holds little back, as well as being richly spiced with wit and humour. She is

Anna Laetitia Aikin (Mrs. Barbauld)
(1743-1825)
Wedgwood plaque – (contemporary)
In Warrington Museum.

the Academy's special covert pupil, since, for her sex, higher education did not exist.

Laetitia was an attractive and personable young lady who set many a heart a-flutter. Her niece Lucy Aikin describes her for us in these words:[12]

> 'She was at this time possessed of great beauty, distinct traces of which she retained to the latest period of life. Her person was slender, her complexion exquisitely fair, with the bloom of perfect health; her features were regular and elegant, and her dark eyes beamed with the light of wit and fancy.'

Thorpe marvels that Joseph Priestley 'Should have left the sprightly, witty Nancy Aikin with the blue and laughing eyes, to be carried off to Palgrave by that queer little man whom she had to honour and obey as a school mistress.' He believes it is 'One of those inscrutable dispensations which the hymeneal gods delight in.' But the fact is that Priestley was already pledged to Mary Wilkinson, whom he married shortly after coming to Warrington. These two young ladies were very close in age and became firm friends throughout their years together about the Academy.

Laetitia captivated a number of young men. Lucy Aikin tells[14] of the first suitor who came a-courting. He was a wealthy young farmer from Kibworth who followed her to Warrington to seek her father's consent to marriage.

> 'My grandfather answered that his daughter was then walking in the garden, and he might go and ask her himself. With what grace the farmer pleaded his cause I know not; but at length out of all patience at his unwelcome importunities, she ran nimbly up a tree which grew by the garden wall, and let herself down into the lane beyond leaving her suitor planté là. The poor man went home disconsolate. He lived and died a bachelor, and though he was never known to purchase any other book whatever, "The Works of Mrs. Barbauld", splendidly bound, adorned his parlour to the end of his days.'

Hamilton Rowan later declared her to have been his first love, though he gives no hint of reciprocation, and although he was at least seven years her junior he was not much younger than his contemporary Barbauld, whom she married. John Howard is also said to have intended a proposal of marriage, but on arrival at a local inn where he was to stay, he was greeted with the news of her engagement, and withdrew from the scene. Jean Paul Marat, who is believed to have been a tutor at the Academy about 1772, is said to have approached her brother to seek his assistance in a proposal, but this is not corroborated.

Apart from Laetitia's own romantic appeal we get a general picture of life at the Academy both from her correspondence and poems. Writing to her cousin Betsy Belsham, one of the Kibworth relatives, with an invitation[15] to visit Warrington she says

> 'We have a knot of lassies just after your own heart, as merry, blithe and gay as you could wish; and very smart and clever.'

Whatever other lassies may have been included, the outstanding members of this little coterie were the two Rigby girls – Sally and Lizzie, the daughters of Mr. and Mrs. John Rigby, who were responsible for housekeeping and the provision of commons to the students, and whose brother Edward was himself a student. (Mrs Rigby was the daughter of Dr. John Taylor.) Laetitia continues[16]

> 'We have a West Indian family too, that I think you would like: a young couple who seem intended by nature for mirth, frolic and gayety. I say nothing of our young men, as I would not flatter you with the hopes of any conquest, for the aforesaid damsels have left no hearts to conquer.'

There is no doubt that the Rigby girls were a sore trial to the tutors, who tried to keep discipline and inculcate sobriety. The situation deteriorated to such a point at one stage that their parents were asked to send them away from home to break the vicious circle of distractions. But in more mature and sober years both were safely married, one of them to a distinguished graduate of the Academy.

It was perhaps to celebrate their return from temporary exile that a party was organised when[17]

> '... they had asked some of the students to supper. Hams and trifles and potted beef were placed before them, and the students were asked to help the ladies. But the hams were made of wood, and the trifles were plates of soap-suds, and the potted beef was potted sawdust, and the other luxuries were equally tempting and equally tantalising.'

Theatrical productions provided another contentious issue between the youthful fervour of students and their supporters on the one hand, and the mature caution of their tutors on the other. Hear Lucy Aikin again:[18]

'Somebody was bold enough to talk of getting up private theatricals. This was a dreadful business! All the wise and grave, the whole tutorhood cried out, "It must not be!". The students, the Rigbys, and, I must add, my aunt, took the prohibition very sulkily, and my aunt's "*Ode to Wisdom*" was the result.'

This short ode[19] is one of Laetitia Aikin's cleverest and most whimsical productions, and just one of those which help to belie Samuel Johnson's disparaging assessment when he thought that her talent was blighted by her non-conformist upbringing. The ode states:

'O Wisdom! if thy soft controul can soothe
the sickness of the soul
Can bid the warring passions cease, and
breathe the calm of tender peace;
Wisdom! I bless thy gentle sway, and ever,
ever will obey.
But if thou com'st with frown austere, to
nurse the brood of Care and Fear;
To bid our sweetest passions die, and leave
us in their room a sigh;

....

Wisdom thine empire I disclaim, thou empty
boast of pompous name!
In gloomy shade of cloisters dwell, but never
haunt my cheerful cell.
Hail to pleasures frolic train! Hail to fancy's
golden reign!
Festive mirth and laughter wild, free and
sportful as the child!
Hope with eager sparkling eyes, and easy
faith and fond surprise!
Let these, in fairy colour drest, for ever share
my careless breast:
Then, though wise I may not be, the wise
themselves shall envy me.'

It is clear from all of this that the atmosphere at Warrington Academy was anything but puritanical; yet Laetitia cannot resist the temptation to indulge her strain of irony. Students might be discouraged from frequenting the local taverns, but given the temperament of many of them, which is revealed in these intimate records, it is unlikely that some of them took the prohibition too literally. However, Laetitia, professing to believe that the ban was absolute, gives reign to her fancy in another tongue-in-cheek poem – 'The Groans of the Tankard'.[20] The speaker in this piece purports to be a tankard in a local ale-house, who looks back to a carefree and joy-filled past, contrasting it with the dour and sober present.

'Twas at the solemn, silent, noon tide hour,
When hunger rages with despotic power,
When the lean student quits his Hebrew roots
For the gross nourishment of English fruits,
And throws unfinished airy systems by
For solid pudding and substantial pie;'

But realising that the liquor with which it was now to be charged was not the gladsome draught to which it had been accustomed the tankard groans –

'How changed the scene! for what unpardoned crimes
Have I survived to these degenerate times?'

It muses o'er the jolly crew it had been wont to serve in times past, then continues –

'Unblest the day, and luckless was the hour,
Which doomed me to a Presbyterian's power:
Fated to serve the Puritanic race,
Whose slender meal is shorter than their grace;
Whose moping sons no jovial orgies keep;
Where evening brings no summons – but to sleep;
No carnival is even Christmas here,
And one long lent involves the meagre year.
Bear me ye powers to some more genial scene
Where on soft cushion lolls the gouty Dean,
Or rosy Prebend with Cherubic face,
With double chin, and paunch of portly grace,
Who lulled in downy slumbers shall agree
To own no inspiration but from me.'

Here she amuses herself by poking fun at the slothful and indulgent among the clergy of the Anglican establishment, in contrast to the sober non-conformist divines.

These distractions at Warrington were no novelty for serious, young, puritan seminarians. Dr. Clegg, who had been a student at Rathmell, commenting on time wasted, recorded in his diary that[21] 'Too much of it was also spent in conversing with the ladies, Mr.

Frankland's daughters, which first led me to read Poetry and Novels and such like trash, which I found reason to wish I had never meddled with.' And John Cockin, visiting Rathmell in 1821, found 'traditions . . . related to the mischievous tricks which the young men played on the country people'.[22]

Another glimpse of the lighter side of life in this Warrington society, is provided by Henry Bright when he states[23] that Rousseau's 'Heloise' had much to answer for. Lucy Aikin had told him that at its appearance 'everybody instantly fell in love with everybody, and then it was that Mr. Barbauld won his bride!' We can imagine a copy of this romantic novel about Heloïse and Abelard, which had been around for a decade or so, finally reaching Warrington and being passed surreptitiously from hand to hand, resulting in the epidemic of romance. Rousseau, had he known, could probably have written an equally romantic novel around this episode. With such characters as Sally and Lizzie Rigby, Anna Laetitia, Rochemont Barbauld, Hamilton Rowan, the Jamaicans and others, he could hardly go wrong!

But there is a more serious side to Laetitia's sentiments which gives us a romantic, but more sober picture of the Academy against its rural backdrop across the river. This comes in a long poem entitled '**The Invitation**'.[24] Again it is addressed to her cousin Betsy Belsham, and may well have been enclosed with the letter of invitation already quoted.

> 'Here gentle summits[a] lift their airy brow;
> Down the steep slope here winds the labouring plough;
> Here, bathed by frequent showers[b] cool vales are seen
> Clothed with fresh verdure and eternal green;[c]

---

a *Hillcliffe.*

b *The weather pattern is familiar.*

c *Some evergreens are still around.*

Here smooth canals,[25a] across the extended plain
    Stretch their long arms to join the distant main:
The sons of toil with many a weary stroke
    Scoop the hard bosom of the solid rock;[b]
Resistless, through the stiff opposing clay[c] . . .

'Cross the lone waste the silver urn they pour,
    And cheer the barren heath or sullen moor.[d]
The traveller with pleasing wonder sees
    The white sail[26] gleaming through the dusky
    trees
And views the altered landscape with surprise,
    And doubts the magic scenes which round him
    rise.
Mark where its simple front yon mansion[e] rears,
    The nursery of men for future years
Here callow chiefs and embryo statesmen lie,
    And unfledged poets short excursions try:
While Mersey's gentle current which too long,
    By fame neglected and unknown to song,
Between his rushy banks, – no poet's theme, –
    Had crept inglorious, like a vulgar stream,
Reflects the ascending seats with conscious pride.
    And dares to emulate a classic tide

....

Where science smiles, the Muses join the train;
    And gentlest arts and purest manners reign.
Ye generous youth who love this studious shade,
    How rich a field is to your hopes displayed!
Knowledge to you unlocks the classic page
    And virtue blossoms for a better age.
How bright the scene to Fancy's eye appears
    Through the long perspective of distant years,

---

a *Sankey and Bridgewater canals.*

b *Local quarries.*

c *Appleton's stodgy clay.*

d *The 'mosses'.*

e *The Bridgefoot Academy.*

When this, this little group, their country calls
    From academic shades and learned halls,
To fix her laws, her spirit to sustain,
    And light up glory through her vast domain!

....

Man is the nobler growth our realms supply,
    And souls are ripened in our northern sky.
Some pensive creep along the shelly shore;
    Unfold the silky texture of a flower;
With sharpened eyes[a] inspect an hornet's sting,
    And all the wonders of an insect's wing.
Some trace with curious search the hidden cause
    Of Nature's changes, and her various laws,
Untwist her beauteous web, disrobe her charms,
    And hunt her to her elemental forms:
Or prove what hidden powers in herbs are found,[b]
    To quench disease and cool the burning wound;
With cordial drops the fainting head sustain,
    Call back the flitting soul, and still the throbs of pain.'

....

This is but a sample. However it reveals with what sensuous charm the young poetess can enumerate the activities of her scholar friends, and set the whole into its natural background. Henry Bright, writing in the mid-nineteenth century is somewhat disparaging about some of the scenic details of the Academy and its surroundings. But it is obvious that he is seeing the scene as it was at this later date and not making allowance for the changes that had by then occurred. An even greater stretch of imagination is required now as the end of the millenium approaches.

Many years after 'The Invitation', **Mrs. Barbauld**, as she then was, returned to this theme when she addressed her 'Epistle to Dr. Enfield – on his revisiting Warrington in 1789'.[27] The Academy had been closed for a number of years and all its people scattered or dead. Enfield had informed the poetess of his visit and this brought memories flooding back. Again there is a fascinating mixture of the

---

a *Microscope.*

b *Medicinal botany.*

serious academic, and the joyful romantic, recapturing, all through, the local scene. She addresses him as

'Friend of those years which from Youth's sparkling fount
With silent lapse down Time's swift gulf have run!'

Laetitia's last four years in Warrington overlapped with Enfield's commencement, but it is doubtful to what extent he might share her enthusiasm for the lighter fantasies. However, they obviously still kept contact, and she would undoubtedly have had a better appreciation of his sentiments at this more mature period in her own life. She was by now in her mid-forties. She pictures him strolling familiar paths on the banks of the Mersey.

'Shades of light transient loves shall pass thee by,
And glowing Hopes, and sports of youthful vein;
And each shall claim one short, half pleasing sigh,
A Farewell sigh to Love's and Fancy's reign.

Lo there the seats where science loved to dwell,
Where liberty her ardent spirit breathed;

....

O seats beloved in vain! Your rising dome
With what fond joy my youthful eyes surveyed;
Pleased by your sacred springs to find my home,
And tune my lyre beneath your growing shade!'

Here she has left the riverside and moved over to the newer buildings in Academy Place, which she well remembers appearing one by one.

'Does desolation spread his gloomy veil
Your grass-grown courts and silent halls along?
Or busy hands there pile the cumbrous sail,
And Trade's harsh din succeed the Muse's song.'

Sail making was a thriving industry in Warrington in those troubled years, and for many years to come, when wars with France engaged the British Navy to the full, and the deserted Academy buildings were acquired by the sail makers for their trade.

'Yet still perhaps in some sequestered walk
Thine ear shall catch the tales of other times;

WA—H

Still in faint sounds the learned echoes talk,
    Where unprofaned as yet by vulgar chimes.

Do not the deeply-wounded trees still bear
    The dear memorial of some infant flame?'

In these flashes she comes across as an incurable romantic, but how vivid are the images; carved initials and other emblems of love cut into the bark of trees in the riverside groves, and yet mixed with the echoes of learned talk!

'Shrouded in stolen glance, here timorous Love
    The grave rebuke of careful Wisdom drew,

Go fling this garland in fair Mersey's stream,
    From the true lovers that have trod his banks;
Say, Thames to Avon still repeats this theme;
    Say, Hymen's captives send their votive thanks.

Visit each shade and trace each weeping rill
    To holy Friendship, or to Fancy known,
And climb with zealous step the fir-crowned hill,
    Where purple foxgloves fringe the rugged
    stone:'

Appleton's Hill-Cliffe was obviously a firm favourite, and small wonder. Even today it unfolds a marvellous panorama; across the Mersey valley to the North, with glimpses as far as the outskirts of Manchester to the East, and Liverpool to the West; then to the foothills of the Pennines, Rivington Pike and Winter Hill, with, when visibility is clearest, the tip of Pendle Hill, away to the North, conveying overtones of magic and witchcraft. Finally the poet has her own fond thoughts of a loved home and family.

'But O the chief! – If in thy feeling breast
    The tender charities of life reside,
If there domestic love have built her nest,
    And thy fond heart a parent's cares divide;

Go seek the turf where worth, where wisdom lies,
    Wisdom and worth, ah, never to return!
There, kneeling, weep my tears, and breathe my sighs,
    A daughter's sorrows o'er her father's urn!'

Laetitia's father is buried in the churchyard of St. Elphin's, and it seems that she never managed to revisit the town herself. But this is no great surprise, in those days when the journey from London, which we undertake so lightly today, was a large adventure, fraught with no little danger. But Enfield was to be her chosen envoy!

The writings of Anna Laetitia, and of Lucy, her niece, have been drawn upon extensively to paint a picture of Warrington in Academy days, though what is here presented is but a small sample of the poet's output. Her complete works are well worth exploring for further insights; and residents of Warrington will find ready access in the local reference library.

Chapter 7
A STILLBORN UNIVERSITY

'The tale is told. The history of Warrington Academy is that of a small, short-lived eighteenth century non-conformist seminary of learning, open to all, struggling to establish principles, methods and ideals, now largely accepted, together with something resembling a modern university education in the midst of a society hostile, when not completely indifferent to its efforts.

During its brief life the Academy attracted to Warrington a circle of scholars and men of letters. The publications of tutors and pupils enjoyed a wide circulation at home and abroad, and have their place in the history of science and literature. Today there is a general acknowledgement of the real worth of the training for commerce and the professions given at Warrington. Its influence may be seen in institutions founded by its tutors and pupils, and in the contribution made to tolerance and liberty as essential to university education.'

McLachlan, 1943.[1]

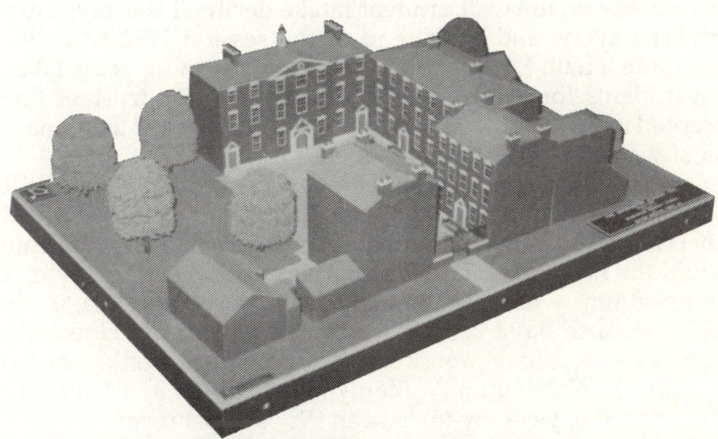

Warrington Academy – purpose built premises in Academy Place. Model presented to town by BNFL.

Right up to the time of Dr. Aikin's death in 1780 the Trustees of Warrington Academy lived in hope. In spite of adversity it had an assured future, they believed. It had the buildings, modest by comparison with the universities, but splendid indeed compared with its predecessors. It had a fine library, respectable scientific apparatus, and most of the resources it needed up to then. Already it had a glorious past, and although its recent reputation was somewhat tarnished, that could be reversed again in a short time. Its students came from far and wide, and if management were to be improved, even more could be recruited. It had been staffed by brilliant men, and even then in Enfield, Wakefield and Clayton it had exceptional scholars. It had, what by then amounted to, its own printing press, that of **William Eyres**,[2] with a splendid array of high class academic publications to its credit. In that very year the trustees were determined to complete their building programme, with one more block which would complete the quadrangle, but this plan was doomed from its conception.

Suddenly, everything fell apart, and Dr. Enfield was perhaps the most immediate cause. Apart from being a fine scholar, he was a dear, gentle, lovable man, who was well regarded by the students, even while they were taking every advantage of the weakness in his temperament. Dr. Aikin had never been Rector; had never been directly responsible for student discipline. He also was gentle and kindly, but withal was made of sterner stuff. Students knew that they could not take advantage of him as long as his health was reasonable, and it remained so up until his final year. He was a prop that Enfield, perhaps unconsciously, had come to lean heavily upon. Then suddenly it was there no more.

The Academy staggered on for another three years,[3] but the writing was on the wall: student intake declined sharply; support withered away, and at the end of the session 1782-83 it finally ground to a halt. Enfield continued for a few more years taking a few students for private tuition, but in 1786 the trustees finally accepted its fate, and wound up the establishment, at the same time transferring the operation to Manchester.

As in so many cases of its kind the causes of collapse were diffuse and it would be quite wrong to pin all the blame on Dr. Enfield. It is necessary to go right back to the early years of the establishment to find the first cause. This was the clash between Dr. Taylor and John Seddon, which has already been described. Originally it might seem to have been but a transient episode. However, in retrospect it was to become a chronic and mortal wound. It eroded support for Warrington Academy and made influential enemies who were always ready to demean the establishment.

It is also remarkable that the financial management over many years was by no means as open as it should have been. Subscribers were not provided with statements of the accounts, which would have enabled them to understand how the venture fared, and might have encouraged them to be more generous. It is well known that if some set an example of generosity others will follow, but the Treasurer does not appear to have appreciated this, and subscriptions were woefully lacking in consequence.

The remuneration of tutors had never been generous. As Lucy Aikin[4] commented, 'The alma mater of Warrington was ever a niggardly recompenser of the distinguished abilities and virtues which were enlisted in her service'.

Lack of discipline with poor management was undoubtedly the major factor, and the evidence of this has already been presented in some detail. The townspeople had suffered in a variety of ways as a result. They were out of patience and would be glad to see the end of the venture. They did not have the breadth of vision to see what its continuation might have meant for the future of the town itself.

Already, as we have seen, there had been rumblings, since the Cromwellian era, about the need for a significant new venture in higher education to challenge and compensate for the deficiencies in the universities, which were maintained by the Church/State establishment, to the exclusion of all dissenters. Warrington Academy in the eighteenth century was the closest the Whig and Non-Conformist opposition ever got to achieving this end.

The Principal of the United College, Bradford (Congregational), commented in 1930:[5]

> 'One of the last dissenting academies in the sense of a school of all the faculties as distinct from a purely theological seminary was that founded at Warrington in 1757 . . . There is a distinctly modern note about the academy, which addressed itself to the education of merchants and bankers, as well as ministers, doctors and lawyers . . . indeed although cut off from the main body of dissent, by its Unitarian association, the academy at Warrington represents the fullest expression of that broader and more humane conception of education which has been the distinctive contribution of puritanism and non-conformity through two centuries.'

This is praise indeed, coming, as it does, from a rival tradition. Its more ardent admirers have spoken of Warrington as 'the first red-brick university' and this it could have been. It might well have been if it had continued its evolution on home ground. It had good buildings in which and from which to develop. It had a revolutionary curriculum and it had outstanding staff. But in moving away it became something else. Its most recent successor – Manchester

College, Oxford, prides itself, and with justification, on having achieved a niche in the 'Holy of Holies'. It has a dignified situation in this glorious university city. It has fine buildings and good resources. It has managed to integrate into the life of the University. But for all that it is only a pale shadow of what Warrington Academy could have become. **It could have been** the first red-brick university half a century before London or Durham, and Warrington might then have become a University city.

One other factor contributing to the downfall, and which has not hitherto been probed, is what might be entitled the 'Unitarian Drift'. Sankey Street Chapel had been Presbyterian from its inception, but during the ministry of John Seddon it became Unitarian, and so it has remained ever since. During the days of the Warrington Academy it was served not only by Seddon, but by those tutors who were ministers, and who supplied for him from time to time. Many of the students worshipped there and so the original local congregation was engulfed.

It is a matter of consequence to ask why some of the most brilliant intellectuals in England at that time should suddenly have adopted Unitarian belief. Priestley was an outstanding example, and as he took such an active and leading part his case is perhaps the best to explore. He had so many interests, but Natural Science was one that certainly engaged a great deal of his time and effort. This was at a time when Science was rapidly emerging from the mumbo-jumbo of medieval mysticism, alchemy and astrology. At last it was becoming wholly rational, and this could be readily demonstrated.

Priestley, as a scientist, and many of his contemporaries with like interests, were themselves firmly grounded in Christianity, unlike some of their intellectual successors in the nineteenth and twentieth centuries, who had drifted, perhaps due to the influence of these earlier peers. As against the rational evolution of Science, Priestley and his associates began to feel uncomfortable with the mysticism which still surrounded their religious heritage, and they felt this too had to be tidied away.

A significant passage occurs in one of Priestley's works, 'A History of the Corruptions of Christianity',[6] where he deals with the traditional Christian doctrine of the Holy Trinity. He writes,

> 'It is very evident that about this time (the end of the second century) the Unitarians were very numerous in all parts of the Christian World; and as they were not distinguished by having assemblies separate from other Christians . . . their opinions certainly could not be deemed *heretical.* It is even acknowledged that many of these Unitarians (*though none of their writings are now come down to us!*) were *men of science*. They are particularly *said to have*

> *been addicted to geometry*, and are also *said to have treated questions in theology in a geometrical method;* but no particulars of this kind are known to us (!) *It is possible* that this circumstance . . . might have arisen from their endeavouring to show, that if the Father, the Son, and the Holy Spirit . . . were each of them God, *in any proper sense of the word*, there must be more Gods than one. Such geometry as this, I doubt not, gave great offence.'

Priestley and his friends had an intellectual dilemma and this piece is largely speculative musing, but a very strange statement to come from the man who considered himself a leading historian in his time at Warrington Academy. He trained his students to be objective; to look for original sources and hard evidence, so how can he justify such a provocative statement entirely without supporting evidence on his own admission, when he says:

> 'It is acknowledged . . . they are said to have been . . . and are said to have treated questions . . . in a geometrical method; but no particulars of this kind are known to us.'

This is special pleading indeed, based on supposition and rumour, no better than the kind of establishment history which he himself would have vigorously refuted in his academic days.

The drift to Unitarianism alienated many who would have been supporters, and even promoters of the project, in other circumstances. Had they not been deterred in this way, a greater corporate interest would have ensured that the problem of discipline was overcome, that a more effective Rector was appointed, with the finances of the institution being clarified and put on a sounder footing. The 'men of the cash book and ledger' would soon have come to appreciate their own stake in this venture, especially for the future education of their own sons, had these issues been effectively addressed. But false starts and unacceptable problems would stultify this development until well into the 19th century, when the new universities began to appear.

Had the Academy continued where it was, it would probably have broadened its intellectual base again; but from its move to Manchester onwards it really became a rather restricted Unitarian establishment, jealously preserving that tradition. Manchester College, Oxford, educates a small number of Unitarian ministers, and in addition has established a fine reputation for itself as a School of Music. It does not have the broad sweep in education which characterised Warrington Academy throughout its life, the curriculum of a whole university rather than just an associate college.

Some desperate attempts were made to salvage the establishment at Warrington.[7] In July 1783 an attempt was made to unite

Warrington Academy with Daventry, with which, as already shown, it had so much in common. It was proposed that Thomas Belsham should have direction of the joint venture, but this move failed, chiefly because the Coward Trust, which supported Daventry, but not Warrington, could not accept the terms of union proposed. This Trust was committed to 'the education of divinity students in a particular way' (which was not Unitarian).

In June 1785 it was suggested that Belsham should leave Daventry to take charge of Warrington Academy, but Belsham himself had reservations about his acceptability. He said, 'I was inclined to do it because I found that my opinions are deviating from orthodoxy, though I had not at that time gone beyond high Arianism. But I thought I was still too orthodox for Warrington.'

Belsham was wrong. He might well have been just the man to revive the Warrington foundation at that time. John Aikin, M.D., who was still teaching part-time at the Academy up to the end, seems not to have been considered for the post of Rector. Yet his heart seems never to have been wholly committed to the practice of medicine; he was much more the academic and literary man, as his subsequent career demonstrates. Perhaps he did not have the stomach for dealing with discipline and management. Yet he appears to have inherited much of his father's temperament, and might well have developed these skills if encouraged to do so.

At this stage the problem degenerates into a speculative game of ifs, buts, and maybes. If Seddon had not had his fatal accident when he did; if the trustees had appreciated that Enfield was not the right man to succeed him as Rector, and had withdrawn him from that role, whilst retaining him as tutor and recruiting a more suitable man for the management; or if a woman had been considered eligible; Anna Laetitia would have managed it better than any of them. She was coping with younger boys excellently at her school in Palgrave, Suffolk, and had the proven capacity to deal with older ones too. But even a century later such an idea would still be unthinkable, and idle speculation will not advance the problem, except to tantalise us further.

Thomas Percival, the Academy's first pupil, was a man of great mettle and not one to indulge in idle fantasies. By now he was a well-established and respected physician in Manchester. Although a trustee of Warrington Academy he was still on the sidelines; much too busy with affairs in the city where he practised, to take a more active interest in his home town and his Alma Mater. But from 1783, when it became obvious that rigor mortis was setting in at Warrington, he began to get more actively involved. At first he would not have wished to be the one to deliver the coup-de-grace, but as the operation came to an end and efforts to revive the corpse successively failed, he began to see the problem in a new light.

There was still a need for the Academy;[8] and Manchester, which was growing fast in both size and national importance, far outstripping Warrington in the process, appeared now to be a more suitable setting. In February 1786 Percival and others proposed the establishment of a Manchester Academy. He was determined to ensure that the effects at Warrington should go to Manchester rather than to the new Hackney College. A steering committee was appointed to launch the new Academy, with Percival as Chairman, and the following resolution was passed,

> 'We whose names are hereunto subscribed (forty-five in all) lamenting the dissolution of the Warrington Academy, disappointed in our expectation of its revival, and persuaded that an institution on the same liberal principles may be established at Manchester, with rational prospects of success, and with great advantages to the cause of learning, virtue, and religion, write in requesting the Rev. Thomas Barnes, D.D. and the Rev. Ralph Harrison to engage in this important undertaking. To promote the execution of it, our intention is to offer a petition to the trustees of that Academy at their Annual meeting in June, for the Loan of the Philosophical and Chemical apparatus, and the library of books now in their possession . . .'

It was deemed the advantages were that no such liberal plan for the education of youth existed within more than a hundred miles.[9] The greater population and the opulence of leading inhabitants of Manchester and district, containing a number of respectable dissenters, would ensure adequate support and enough pupils. Other advantages mentioned were: good policing in the town, which it was hoped would discourage unruly students; access to the superb library at Chetham's Hospital, which had been one of the attractions for the first Manchester Academy in 1698; and a new feature, that students intending a career in medicine would be able to attend for tuition at the Infirmary.

A final meeting of the trustees took place in Warrington on June 29th, at which twenty-four were present, including Percival.[10] This meeting was in favour of dissolution, and all the trustees were then balloted. Fifty-four voted for dissolution, of whom seventeen were among those who had signed the invitation to Barnes and Harrison at Manchester, and twelve became members of the new committee of trustees. It was decided that money resulting from the sale of the Warrington buildings should be equally divided between Manchester and Hackney. The library was to go to Manchester and the scientific apparatus to Hackney. It was November 1838 before the buildings were finally sold, by which time Hackney College was long since defunct. After clearing debts, £117 was paid over to the

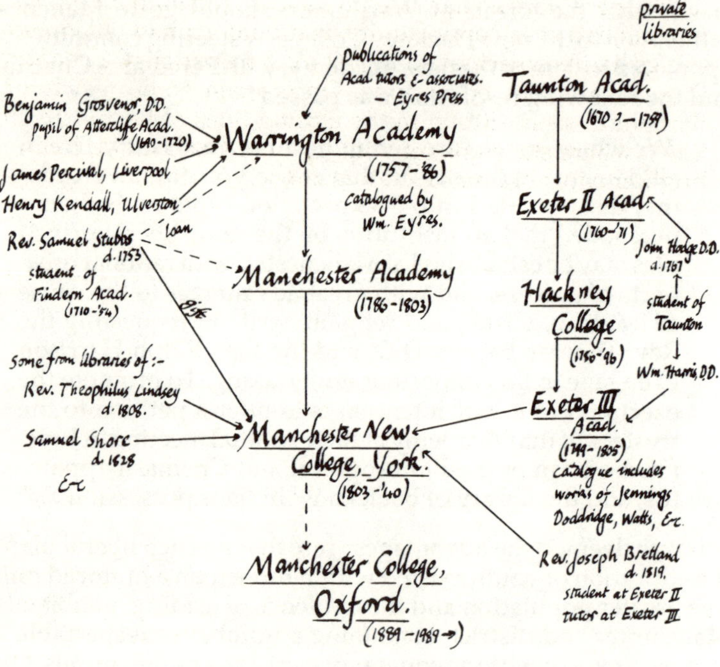

University Hall London housed Manchester College (1853-1859) now Dr. Williams's Library.

trustees of Manchester College, which is the only payment recorded.

Everything had been conducted with due decorum. The several moves to salvage the Academy at Warrington had proceeded without any outside pressure, before the bid came from Manchester. So there were no hard feelings and no recriminations. Warrington had had every opportunity, and finally it had failed, but great things had been achieved in just over a quarter of a century, and those would not be undone. Once again some words of Mrs. Barbauld[11] seem fitting, in the closing lines of her poem entitled 'Life', where she signs off with 'Say not Good night, but in some brighter clime bid me Good morning'.

Chapter 8
SUCCESSORS

'In proportion as men go honestly down into the depths of their own nature, and listen to the voice of God which speaks within, they will be drawn closer to one another, and feel the uniting effects of Divine communion. We will not, then, devote our College to any such negative and transient purpose as protesting against the supposed errors of others, or twitting them with what may seem to us the fetters that bind them, but, according to its fundamental rule, we will consecrate it to promote the study of Religion, Theology and Philosophy; and we will seek ever for ourselves, and for all whom we can influence, a higher learning, a deeper faith and a more devoted love.'

Rev. James Drummond, 1891.[1]

Cross Street chapel, Manchester, built 1694, destroyed by bombing in Second World War. Many academy associations (see chart), replaced with new building in 1959.

Warrington Academy was no more, and the action shifted back again to **Cross Street Chapel, Manchester**,[2] which has been a constant link in this story from first to last. John Chorlton (1666-1705) had been a pupil at Frankland's Rathmell Academy. He came to Manchester in 1687 as assistant to Henry Newcome, the minister who had been ejected from the Collegiate church (later to become Manchester Cathedral) whom he succeeded in 1695. Three years later Chorlton founded the first Manchester Academy, where he was assisted by James Coningham, who had come as his joint pastor in 1700 to the Cross Street Chapel. Coningham's successor, Eliezer Birch[3] was another Rathmell graduate, and his successor Joseph Mottershead was a graduate of Attercliffe Academy under Timothy Jollie. John Seddon, who came as Mottershead's assistant in 1741, had been a Kendal student.

The next three ministers at Cross Street were all Warrington Academy men: Robert Gore who succeeded Seddon from 1770-79, Ralph Harrison who joined him as his assistant in 1771 and Thomas Barnes, who joined Harrison in 1780 after Gore's death. It was these two, Harrison and Barnes, who were to be the first tutors at the new Manchester Academy. Their successor, John Grundy, was one of the graduates of that Academy, and so the links were to continue down through the nineteenth century until the final move to Oxford, with John Gooch Robberds and William Gaskell, students at York and Professors back at Manchester. Then James Drummond, a Dublin graduate, who became a student at Manchester College in London, going on to become a Professor there and Principal in the final years before the College moved to Oxford, where he was the first Principal. His son, William Hamilton Drummond, was a London pupil, who later ministered at Cross Street, then Cairo Street, Warrington, before moving to Belfast in 1900.

There is a remarkable association between Cross Street Chapel ministers and the particular group of academies reviewed in this book, which is set out in even greater detail in the accompanying chart.

With the collapse of Warrington Academy there was no longer any doubt about Manchester's pre-eminent claim to succession. This city was gaining all the advantages with growth in population, industry, trade, power and influence. Its Rational Dissenters were a strong, self-confident and well organised group whose principal focus at the time was the Cross Street Chapel.[4] From the time of John Seddon's ministry (1741-69) onwards there was no doubt about its Unitarian bent, but in spite of this dominance, when the new Academy was founded it was firmly stated that 'This institution will be open to young men of every religious denomination, from whom no test, or confession of faith will be required.' At the same time the special interest of English Protestant Presbyterian Dissenters or Non-subscribing Dissenters is identified. Thomas Barnes in his opening public address at the beginning of the first session dedicated the Academy 'To Truth, To Liberty, To Religion', a slogan which is now inscribed on Manchester College, Oxford.

The new establishment was, to a remarkable extent, an extension of the Warrington foundation, with **Thomas Barnes** and **Ralph Harrison** for tutors, who were both Warrington graduates, as was the President – Dr. Thomas Percival. The library and archives of Warrington Academy were also transferred to Manchester, whilst the scientific equipment was sent to the other newly established college at Hackney. The first students had their classes in the chapel room at Cross Street, but soon they moved to larger premises on what is now Mosley Street behind the Town Hall. (This building has long since gone.) An outstanding tutor was the Quaker, **John Dalton**[5] (1793-1800) who was, like Priestley, a pioneer in Chemistry. This Academy ran into the same problems as Warrington with student indiscipline, and it is at this stage that **George Walker**, who had previously been a tutor at Warrington Academy, was brought in from Nottingham where he had been a minister for twenty-four years. He was sixty-three years of age and his subsequent career at Manchester was no more happy nor successful than Taylor's had been at Warrington. **William Stevenson**, a Scotsman, was tutor in Classics. His daughter Elizabeth was to achieve fame in later years as Mrs. Gaskell, the novelist, when married to another tutor in a later phase of the college's history.

Contemporary with Manchester Academy was the short-lived **Hackney College**[6] with its turbulent history. It is not in the direct line of succession we are considering, but it is a close offshoot and merits attention, more because of its significance in terms of national politics than for any academic distinction it acquired. It was born in the time of great social and intellectual ferment which brought the Revolution in France, with much associated political upheaval in England, Scotland and Ireland. The British establishment under George III and William Pitt was feeling threatened and the last thing it needed was a focus for unwelcome ideals right at the heart of the nation, so Hackney was not welcome.

This new establishment had much in common with the academies at Warrington and Daventry. When a new model was being planned in the 1750s the chosen site was to be well away from the capital, but now this was history. In spite of the failure at Warrington and the problems at Daventry the time was considered ripe for a new venture in London itself. With the closure of Hoxton, liberal dissenters had no other resort in the capital, and little choice elsewhere. There is no doubt as to its bias, but at the same time it does not perhaps merit Irene Parker's description[7] as 'definitely denominational'. It was not exclusive, any more than Warrington had been, or Manchester was to be. In 1792 Priestley notes that[8] 'One gentleman of the Roman Catholic persuasion, and several of the Church of England were then in residence'.

Why was the title changed to College? The answer is provided by one of the tutors. 'This term was used not for the sake of imitating the Establishment, but because the word Academy (applied of late to every common school) does not convey a proper idea of our plan of education.'[9]

Like Warrington and Daventry there was to be a group of tutors each with a different brief. Again most of them were ministers, but this time they continued to minister to their congregations in neighbourhoods round about, so they were not full-time academics, reverting in this respect to the old pattern. In the short time of its existence there was a rapid turnover in tutors, reflecting perhaps the general instability of the time.

At the start there were four tutors, soon enlarged to six and in ten years, with turnover, there were thirteen in all. Among the founders was **Richard Price**, D.D.(Aberdeen) and LL.D.(Yale), the friend of Benjamin Franklin, Joseph Priestley and Theophilus Lindsey. He was minister at the Gravel Pit, Hackney, and Newington Green. His special interest was mathemathics, in particular the subject of Chances and Life-Annuities, being one of the first expert advisers to some of the early insurance companies. He also lectured on the Discoveries of Sir Isaac Newton. But he was drawing to the end of his life and not in good health, rather like John Taylor at Warrington, though with less dire consequences. He resigned his tutorship in the second year and died a few years later.

With the closure of the Academy at Daventry, **Thomas Belsham** came on to Hackney in the same year, 1789. He taught theology, Hebrew and shorthand. He was critical of the education offered in these and other academies, stating that the courses, because of their breadth, tended to superficiality.

Gilbert Wakefield, the Cambridge scholar, who had been a late tutor at Warrington Academy, came to Hackney in 1790 to teach classics, but due to the cantankerous streak in his nature he 'got across' his colleagues and left again after only one year, to be succeeded by John Pope who had been a pupil at Exeter.

Priestley, after he lost his home in the Birmingham riots, came on to London. He offered his services free to the College, where he lectured on History and General Policy as at Warrington, and also on Natural Philosophy, a challenge which he would have much enjoyed at Warrington.

Among the **pupils** was **William Hazlitt**, the essayist, who has left us various comments on the establishment; Arthur Aikin, the son of John from Warrington, and grandson of the Kibworth John

Aikin. Arthur was to become a geologist and later secretary to the Society of Arts. **Charles Wellbeloved** came on from Homerton Academy where he was unhappy with its strict Calvinism. Afterwards he settled at York, and in 1803 he became Principal of Manchester College when the Academy closed and the establishment moved to York. Another student, Jeremiah Joyce, was arrested in 1794 for his radical sympathies. He was kept in gaol from May until October, when he was tried with other members of the London Societies and acquitted.

Students and tutors were much in harmony in their radical sympathies and attitudes to events in France. In 1789 Dr. Price was invited by the Revolution Society, which was commemorating the centenary of the Glorious (English) Revolution, to preach a sermon at the Old Jewry. He took as his title 'A Discourse on the Love of Our Country'. The establishment considered the discourse to be inflammatory, though most neutral observers would deem it mild and reasonable. However, it provoked Edmund Burke's famous 'Reflections on the Revolution in France', which was quite reactionary and was to become the standard around which the establishment rallied.

Priestley, who was still settled at Birmingham, preached a sermon to supporters of the College in April 1791 which, like Price's, irritated the establishment, and there were thoughts of proceeding against him. This was followed by a pamphlet written by a student of the College and circulated in Birmingham, which inflamed feelings in the weeks leading up to the riot in July when Priestley lost his home and his chapel.[10]

In the summer of 1792 there was a Republican Supper in Hackney College at which Tom Paine was a guest of honour. A few years earlier students had been at Westminster Hall for the trial of Warren Hastings, and in 1790, 'they had flocked to the gallery of the House of Commons on the night when Charles James Fox, arriving booted and spurred from Newmarket, delivered his two great speeches in favour of the Repeal of the Test and Corporation Acts'.[11]

With all this ferment, the writing was on the wall. Liberal Dissenters began to take fright, and withdrew their support. Price had died in 1791; Thomas Rogers, chairman of the committee, in 1793; and Dr. Kippis, the longest serving tutor, in 1795. Priestley had emigrated to America in 1794. Quickly the collapse came, and the College closed in 1796.

McLachlan sums it up as follows:[12]

> 'Its premature fate dismayed Unitarians and delighted their adversaries, and evoked a fine passage from Thomas Belsham, its principal tutor. "The spirit of the times was

> against it; it fell – and the birds of night, ignorance and envy, bigotry and rancour, screamed their ungenerous triumph over the ruins of this stately edifice; whilst virtue, truth and learning mourned in secret over the disappointment of their fond hopes and of their too highly elevated expectation".'

The library which had come from the second Exeter Academy supplemented by that of Dr. William Harris, passed back to Exeter in its next phase and later went to Manchester College, York, from which it eventually reached Oxford.

The Academy at Manchester seems to have been a rather low key affair, and it ended at the beginning of the nineteenth century. But there would still be continuity. There was no one at Manchester to revive the project,[13] although there had been an attempt again to induce Thomas Belsham, who was available once more after the collapse of Hackney College, to take it on, but without success. William Turner, the Warrington graduate settled at Newcastle-upon-Tyne was also approached, but although he afforded much support to the institution in the years ahead he was not prepared to commit himself to it full-time and move from where he had settled. Eventually the **Rev. Charles Wellbeloved at York** was prevailed upon to undertake the task. However he was not prepared to come to Manchester, and so for the next thirty-seven years **Manchester College**, as it was thenceforward called, flourished at York. Wellbeloved, a native of London, educated there at Homerton Academy and Hackney College, was Minister at St. Saviours-gate Chapel. By his marriage to Ann Kinder, the daughter of Anna Laetitia Jennings, he became involved in the Kibworth dynasty - the Jennings, the Aikins and the Belshams. He lived at 38, Monkgate, at the back of which he built a schoolroom, which later housed the library. In 1811 separate college premises were acquired across the road, comprising a lecture hall, to which classrooms were later added at the back. Sound investments at this stage put the College in a much more secure position than its predecessors, but the fees charged to lay students were still expected to subsidise the clerics.

An interesting development at York[14] was initiated by the students themselves, who asked permission to go out preaching into some of the surrounding villages, to help them prepare for the ministry. This venture met with considerable success, and echoed Doddridge's scheme at Northampton.

Many notable names[15] occur in the records of that period, but only a few will be considered. The first is **James Martineau**, who was a student in the early twenties, and was involved when the College changed location again in the late thirties. **William Turner**, son of the Warrington graduate already referred to, was a student at York, went on to Glasgow University and then Edinburgh before returning to York to serve for eighteen years as tutor in 'Mathematics with Natural and Experimental Philosophy'. **William Hincks** was born in Cork where his father was a minister and lecturer in the Royal Cork Institution. He was a student of Turner at York and then in 1827 became his successor.

The tutor closest to Wellbeloved was **John Kenrick**,[16] who came to York in 1810 and remained to the end. Born at Exeter in 1788, he was educated in the Academy which his father conducted in that city, going afterwards to Glasgow University. In 1819-20 he obtained leave of absence to spend a sabbatical year abroad pursuing his studies in Classics and History. The winter semester he spent at Göttingen and the following summer at Berlin. After eleven years in the post he married Wellbeloved's eldest daughter Laetitia, thus allying himself, at one further remove, to the Kibworth clan. After the College moved back to Manchester in 1840 he joined the staff there.

Davis reports that 'Yorkists' had the reputation in after years of solid learning. He quotes Kenrick as saying that 'The object of this institution is not to make preachers, but scholars.' (The reverse of Jollie at Attercliffe.) He quotes further from Charles Beard's centenary address:[17]

> 'The students, never very numerous, were a little community apart, of which every member was known to every other; bound together by common faith and purpose; somewhat isolated in the midst of an old and aristocratic cathedral city, the life of which touched them, while they formed no part of it.'

The College at York had 235 students in all. Unlike its predecessors the clerical students outnumbered the lay by 122 to 113. So the average intake was just over six per year, and the average in residence about twenty-five per year. Among the lay students were many who became leaders in commerce, industry and public life. Beard, in the same address, speaks of them as[18]

> 'Men who, not ashamed of their nonconformity, held the outposts of conscientious conviction stoutly yet in all charity and courtesy; to whom the principles of civil and religious liberty were as the very breath of their nostrils; who were the ardent advocates of every social and political reform; and full of a fine public spirit, showed themselves the salt of the communities in which they lived.'

It was still Manchester College, and its base in that city was not forgotten. When the Jubilee came to be celebrated in 1836 it was with services in the Cross Street Chapel and a formal dinner at Hayward's Hotel. It was also becoming clear that the time at York was drawing to a close. In 1839 Wellbeloved was seventy years of age and Kenrick was in poor health, so the question was posed whether to return to Manchester or move to London. James Martineau was commissioned to present a case to the Committee for removal back to Manchester, and John James Tayler, another old pupil who, since 1822, had been the clerical secretary, was to present a case for moving to London.

In 1828 London University had been founded,[19] and many believed that the College should migrate to the capital, especially when the Royal Charter of 1836 guaranteed access without any religious test. (This was still an obstacle at Oxbridge.) There would be greater teaching potential, as well as ready access to the metropolitan libraries and museums. Those favouring Manchester argued that there students preparing for the ministry would be in closer touch with the vigorous non-conformity of the North. The committee voted narrowly in favour of Manchester!

And so back they came, in close connection once more with Cross Street Chapel, but a link with London was also forged. A Warrant was granted to **Manchester New College**[20] to issue certificates to candidates for degrees in the University of London.

The original Royal Warrant establishing the new University had stated that it was

> 'For the advancement of Religion and Morality, and the promotion of useful knowledge, to hold forth to all classes and denominations, without any distinction whatever, an encouragement for pursuing a religious and liberal course of education, to confer the distinctions justly due to proficiency in Literature, Science or Art *without imposing a Test of Religious opinions.*'

Most significantly it was declared

> 'Expedient to extend the benefits of Colleges already instituted, whether incorporated or unincorporated, by connecting them with the said University.'

Back at Manchester premises were provided at Grosvenor Square, but as time passed it came to be regarded as a temporary station, especially in 1857 when a rival establishment, **Owen's College,**[21] was launched, which in time was to become Manchester University. Once again the Academy had missed its chance to become the University. In spite of problems the College in this latest phase had its successes, and some distinguished staff. Eight Professors were appointed, three for Divinity, five for Literature and Science. **James Martineau** was Professor of Philosophy and Political Economy. He lived at Liverpool, where he served as Minister to the Paradise Street Chapel, and commuted to Manchester by rail once a week. **William Gaskell** was clerical secretary and Professor of English Literature, a department in which he might well have been overshadowed by his more famous literary wife; herself the daughter of William Stevenson, who had been Classics tutor in the first Manchester period. Gaskell was born in Warrington, of a long established non-conformist family, which worshipped at the Sankey Street Chapel, and which at that time was engaged in manufacturing and supplying coarse sailcloth for the Navy. **Francis Wm. Newman**, the younger brother of John Henry, and also an Oxford graduate, was Professor of Classics and English Language. **Rev. John Gooch Robberds**, of Huguenot stock, a York graduate, and Minister at Cross Street Chapel, was appointed Professor of Pastoral Theology and Semitic Languages. **Rev. John J. Tayler**, another York graduate, became Professor of Ecclesiastical History, and was minister at Upper Brook Street Chapel. **Rev. Robert Wallace**, another York student, was Professor of Theology and Biblical Archaeology. When Wallace retired from the College he was succeeded by **George Vance Smith**, yet another York student. **Kenrick** also followed on from York as Professor of Ancient and Modern History and the History of Literature. **Robert Finlay**, a Dublin University graduate, was Professor of Mathematics.

The premises at Grosvenor Square[22] were further from the centre of Manchester than the earlier Academy had been, and this time there was no residential accommodation; the students living in lodgings approved by the committee. A social focus was provided for students by William and Elizabeth Gaskell, in a somewhat similar way to that afforded by the Aikins at Warrington. One of the students recorded in later years how they had enjoyed 'frequent, personal, friendly intercourse with Mrs. Gaskell,' and had 'charming memories of country walks with her, and frequent evenings in her company.' Gooch Robberds also used to entertain students by having them to his home for Shakespearean readings.

During these thirteen years at Manchester[23] there were sixty students in all, thirty-two clerical and twenty-eight lay. Many of them had distinguished careers in after life; three, who were journalists, became editors of 'The Spectator', the 'Manchester Guardian' and the 'Daily News' respectively. Robert Darbishire became lay secretary to the College in London, and held the post for thirty-seven years into the Oxford period. Charles Beard was clerical secretary for twenty-two of those years in London.

During the final years at Manchester an interesting debate was taking place as to whether there should be sectarian education at

Owen's College or in the schools. J.J.Tayler, in a letter to the 'Manchester Guardian', posed the question and gave his own answer.[24]

> 'How then is religious instruction, which the course of scientific teaching provided for all inevitably excluded, to be collaterally supplied? No plan so obviously just and practicable suggests itself, as that different religious bodies should supply out of their resources, in halls specially opened for the purpose, courses of lectures on the chief topics of theology and ecclesiastical history and religious philosophy, in which the subject should be distinctly presented from their own point of view, and set forth earnestly in accordance with their peculiar principles. The clustering of many such schools of religious learning around a common scientific centre, growing out of the deep heart and nourished by the spontaneous energy and zeal of different churches, would be a far nobler homage to religion, and tend far more to diffuse its power and blessing, than a formal provision and void of all character and earnestness, which could not meet the wants of all and might infringe the consciences of some; and though such an arrangement has, at first view, a sectarian aspect, it would contribute in the final result more than any other method to remove the causes of sectarianism and to encourage a genuine catholicity of spirit.'[25]

This now looks like an interesting prevision of what would come about in many universities in future years, Manchester itself being a good example.

As foreseen the move to London had merely been delayed. A significant new development was the establishment of University Hall in London, at Gordon Square, to commemorate the passing of the Dissenters' Chapels Act of 1844. It was set up to provide 'instruction in theology, mental and moral philosophy, and other branches of knowledge not at all, or not fully, taught at University College.'[26] It was also to provide living accommodation for students under a resident Principal. Here then was the magnet which would finally bring Manchester College to London. However, a succession of reports, debates and votes still lay ahead until, at the end of 1852 a resolution was carried 'that the College should be moved to London, as a theological institution, in connection for literary and scientific purposes, with University College.'

In 1853 Manchester College moved to University Hall,[27] thus strengthening the association already established at the beginning of the last phase. For the first time Manchester College, with its rich heritage, drawn from a broad representative section of the earlier dissenter academies, and their tradition of free enquiry, had a foothold within a university. This latest academic acknowledgment of freedom to enquire, and freedom to challenge, was not of course welcomed by some orthodox Christian establishments. It was only too easy to summon up a host of bogey-men from the French Revolution onwards to put a brake on the 'freethinkers'. Freewill was a basic tenet of traditional Christianity, but the free exercise of that will by academic bodies or individuals was a different matter. 'Establishment' had never, did not then, and probably never will welcome too much probing. It is faithfully wedded to the 'status quo ante'.

But the significant fact is that a great breakthrough was occurring which encouraged rational enquiry across the board, from physical science to scriptural study and theology, unencumbered by slavish adherence to tradition. This would lead to excess and folly at times, but not more so than in the past and among traditionalists themselves. In the main it was to bring tremendous progress, and if not all of that was applied for the greater good of humanity as a whole, this is only because of the exercise of that free will which Christianity so readily acknowledges, but which can be applied for good or ill.

In 1854, the year after the College left Manchester, the Unitarian Home Missionary College[28] was established there; but although there has been an element of rivalry the two institutions have worked in reasonable harmony. The new College in London was never without its problems, some of which harked back to earlier times, such as those of resident students and discipline, the balance of lay and clerical students, and financial support; but none of these threatened the continuity of the establishment to the extent that they had done in the past. However, in a new age of affluence and freedom for dissenters it was more difficult to get young men of good family to commit themselves to the lowly vocation of ministry, with its poor reward in worldly terms, when they could take up exciting and much more remunerative challenges in civil life.

Nevertheless the College did grow in strength, being well staffed and enjoying firm leadership. It started with two full-time Professors.[29] **J.J.Tayler** was Principal, and had the chair of Doctrinal and Practical Theology with Ecclesiastical History. **Vance Smith** was Professor of Critical and Exegetical Theology, Evidences of Religion and Semitic Languages. Its outstanding teacher and ultimate leader was **James Martineau**. For the first few years he continued his ministry at Liverpool and served the College part-time as lecturer in Philosophy. On every other Monday he travelled to London – the College was near Euston Station. He lectured for two days, and on the second day returned home, a remarkable example of one of the earliest long-distance railway commuters.[30] After four years Vance Smith resigned, and it was proposed to appoint Martineau to the vacancy. However, there was a reaction among some of the trustees. Apparently he was not a sufficiently orthodox Unitarian, and the same criticism was made of Tayler, the Principal.

This problem had first arisen in 1839 during the Liverpool Unitarian controversy,[31] with Martineau's lecture entitled 'The Christian View of Moral Evil', in which he had protested against Hartley's doctrine of 'Philosophical Necessity', enshrined and handed down by Priestley and Belsham, and which he himself had taught until then. When he had cast it off he described his emancipation as 'an inward deliverance from artificial system into natural speech; . . . an escape from a logical cage into the open air.'[32] Ellery Channing, writing to Martineau in 1840 to express his satisfaction, said he had 'felt that this doctrine, with its natural connections, was a mill-stone round the neck of Unitarianism in England.' He went on to add, 'I have always lamented that Dr. Priestley's authority had fastened this doctrine on his followers.'[33]

Some of the trustees were concerned about the possible exclusion by Tayler and Martineau of views on the controversy regard-

James Martineau statue in front of the Warrington Window, commemorating trustees, staff and students of Warrington Academy in the library of Manchester College, Oxford.

ing 'Evidences of Natural and Revealed Religion', not shared by them.[34] A special committee was appointed to consider the problem and report, but eventually the objections were voted down by 113 to 17.[35] A further resolution stressed that it was the tradition of their institution to provide teaching 'without test or confession of faith and not for the purpose of instruction in the peculiar doctrines of any sect.' This statement harks back to the charges which John Taylor had given to his students when Warrington Academy was established, and to the broader sentiments of Joseph Priestley.

The decision was a happy one, as Martineau continued to serve the College for many years, and latterly as Principal. When he died in 1900 he was in his ninety-fifth year, having taught in the College for forty-five of those years. When he retired he was elected President for the next two years, which included the Centenary in 1886. That he was greatly revered by his students is reflected by the many glowing tributes which were paid to him in those later years, and when he died. His outstanding contribution is commemorated by the fine statue in white marble which dominates the library at Oxford. It shows him seated in his chair as his students would have seen him when he lectured.

In 1871 Parliament finally abolished the Confessional Tests which barred Dissenters from Oxford and Cambridge; thus undoing the mischief of more than two centuries. Around that time doubts began to be expressed about the connection with University College,[36] and a system of undergraduate exhibitions was adopted, by which students were enabled to graduate at some other University than London, and to come to the College only for their theological course. A committee was appointed in 1875 which studied the developing situation in some depth, and eventually in 1879 presented the trustees with three options and the case which might favour each one. The first was to remain in London. The second was to move to Oxford or Cambridge, and the third was to return to Manchester. Although there were a few who strongly favoured a return to Manchester, it was immediately obvious that this would not be supported by a significant number, and so the contest was between supporters of Oxford and those who would choose to remain in London. Eventually the decision was in favour of London by a two to one majority, which meant that the final move was postponed for another decade.

During this time the financial position of University Hall was not good.[37] So in 1881 Manchester College made an extra payment of £250 in return for additional student accommodation. Later a new scheme gave the College full responsibility for management. Thereafter the property was vested in a new body of trustees, half from the College and half from the Society of University Hall. The new Trust Deed virtually handed over the Hall to the College, because, when and if the property was disposed of, the Trust Fund would accrue to the College.

During the final years in London, after Martineau's resignation, he was succeeded as Principal by one of his former pupils – Dr. **James Drummond**,[38] who was a graduate in Classics from Trinity College, Dublin; and in Divinity from London. He had ministered for a time at Cross Street Chapel, Manchester, before he joined the College staff in London. Another student in later years was his son William Hamilton Drummond, who also came to minister at Cross Street Chapel, and later at Cairo Street Chapel in Warrington.

It was in London that women students first appeared in the College,[39] unofficially at first at Martineau's lectures, at the time when London University degrees were first open to women. After a prolonged wrangle in committee over a two year period, it was finally decided at a meeting of Trustees in 1876 that women should officially be admitted, but it was not until 1901 that the first woman was accepted into the full course of training for the ministry; she was already a graduate of St. Andrews.

In the late eighties a proposal to remove to Oxford came again.[40] The debate was keen and the voting close, with numerous meetings of committee and of trustees. At a meeting in Manchester in January 1889, with sixty-nine trustees present, a resolution in favour of Oxford was carried by thirty-four votes to seven, but it was decided to hold a postal ballot of all the trustees. This time the voting was closer, at 138 to 109, but Oxford had won! University Hall was sold to the trustees of **Dr. Williams's library**,[41] thus keeping it in the tradition of liberal non-conformity.

After more than two centuries, dissenting English Protestants could return again to Oxford, to establish a free school of Theology, a place of training for ministers of religion on the open principle, free from all dogmatic constraint. Temporary accommodation was acquired at 90, High Street,[42] while a permanent home was planned and erected. A piece of ground was purchased from Merton College at the corner of Holywell Street and what was to become Mansfield Road. The old houses fronting this on Holywell were purchased for College residences. One of these was named Rathmell House and another Warrington House, stressing earlier associations.

A fear, expressed by Martineau and others,[43] who had opposed the move, was that the College would remain isolated from the life of the University as a whole, but this has not been so. There was an immediate warm welcome from outstanding academic leaders like Jowett, the Master of Balliol. The Principal, Doctor James Drummond, was a graduate of Trinity College, Dublin, which, as an Elizabethan foundation, had reciprocity with Oxford and Cambridge. Thus, in his own person he was a link between two different traditions, and this was an immediate bonus. In the year preceding the move an Honorary D.C.L. had been conferred on Martineau, and in 1901 Rev. J. Estlin Carpenter, the Vice-Principal, was awarded an Honorary M.A.. In 1920, when degrees in Divinity were made open by the University, he took the Oxford D.D.. From the first, students of Manchester College had the advantage of being able to attend lectures by many distinguished University men, some of whom were able to assist the College in a variety of practical ways.

Martineau, and others who had opposed the Oxford move, were unstinting in their support once the decision had been taken. Of the new buildings erected the chapel and the library were to become the special glories. The windows in the chapel are especially beautiful, being the work of William Morris, with designs by Burne-Jones. The large window over the communion table was a gift of Frederick Nettlefold, another of the opposers.

In Warrington a fund was established[44] by the minister and congregation at Cairo Street Chapel for a window to grace the library. This commemorates the Warrington Academy, its tutors, its Presidents and one distinguished lady associate – Mrs. Barbauld. The group from Warrington which came to make this presentation, was led by the minister, **Rev. William Hamilton Drummond**, and the gift was formally received by the Principal, Doctor James Drummond (his father).[45] Even more important than the window however, is the library itself, incorporating the books of the Warrington Academy, which came at last to rest after their wanderings for more than a century, through Manchester, York and London.

There is one feature in the history of the College which must strike an odd note with any outsider, in view of the strong and repeated protestations of radical liberalism.[46] A recurrent and somewhat strident Unitarian orthodoxy surfaces from time to time when its ethos in any way appears to be threatened. In 1891 on the day when the stone was laid for the new building, the opening address to the students was given by a well-known broad Churchman. This displeased a number of influential trustees, who took the committee to task. Their reply was an emphatic vindication of consistency.

However, where appointing a member of the permanent teaching staff was concerned, the outcome was not always so liberal or so generous. In later days in London Martineau and Drummond favoured the appointment of Colenso, another broad Churchman, to the chair of Old Testament studies, but the committee decided against them.[47] Martineau's comment is significant. He said, 'I do not see that our own rule of abstinence from tests obliges us to set up a test against tests!' This is not surprising from a man whose own appointment, so many years before, had been in doubt for a season.

The strangest case of all was that of William Addis,[48] who got the Old Testament studies appointment in 1899. He was brought up as a Presbyterian, the son of a minister, but became Roman Catholic in his twenties. Twenty-seven years later he became Unitarian, and served as minister at Nottingham. From there he came to the College, but after a few years he decided that his true refuge was with the Anglican communion. This final move was a considerable embarrassment to the College hierarchy, and a cause of dissension; but he was allowed to continue in the post for another six years.

Even professed adherents sometimes veered away from Unitarian orthodoxy in a remarkable fashion. Andrew Fuller,[49] comparing the Calvinistic and Socinian systems, states that, 'Socinianism, while it divests the gospel of all that is interesting and affecting to the souls of men, substitutes nothing in its place. If it be Christianity at all, it is, as *the ingenious Mrs. Barbauld* is said in time past to have expressed it – *Christianity in the frigid zone.*'

English and American education owe much to this 'alternative tradition', as it has been called. Even among the establishments that have been noted many fine and distinguished individuals, supporters, tutors and graduates have been passed over. Greater detail can be found in the sources which have been quoted. Family tradition has been notable throughout, and some particular examples have already been given. But to savour its strength one more is offered; that of the Turner family, two members of which have already been mentioned.

Library Quadrangle at Manchester College, Oxford.

John Turner (1689-1737) was educated at the first Manchester Academy. In 1712 he became Minister at Walton Chapel, near Preston. In 1715 he joined the Army to resist the Old Pretender, and was commended for his leadership by the Hanoverian General. His son, William Turner (1714-94) was educated at Findern Academy and Glasgow University, continuing the family tradition. His son, also William Turner (1761-1859), was educated at Warrington Academy, and was its first historian. He settled at Newcastle-upon-Tyne, where he helped to found one of the most outstanding Literary and Philosophical Societies.[50] He was actively engaged in the work of Manchester College at York and Manchester as official visitor for many years. His son, again William Turner (1788-1853) was tutor at York; a truly remarkable family succession.

Chapter 9
POSTSCRIPT

'Is a danger to be trusting one another
One will seldom want to do what other wishes
But unless someday somebody trusts somebody
There'll be nothing left on earth excepting fishes.'
The King and I. (Rodgers and Hammerstein)

It should be obvious from this study that English Dissenters are, in the main, far from being narrow-minded, ignorant, puritanical, kill-joys, as so often portrayed. If popular history is fossilised propaganda then an autocratic establishment will never be happy with people of independent views, who have the moral courage to withstand its pressures. On the other hand good souls will never be lacking, prepared to sacrifice all to uphold their beliefs and forever seek justice.

Injustice in one form or another is to be found in every land, but at present we have to look further afield for its grosser manifestations, to a Nelson Mandela, an Alexander Solzhenitsyn, and many more besides. England had its heroic sons in times past, like John Bunyan or Sir Thomas More. Of the characters here reviewed Joseph Priestley may be cited who, towards the end of a long life of service to humanity, was beset by the mob which destroyed his chapel, his home, his family's goods and chattels, his scientific apparatus, his books and papers; much that was irreplaceable. King George III, when told of the outrage, could only say, 'As the mischief did occur, it was impossible not to feel pleased at its having fallen on Priestley rather than another, that he might feel the wickedness of the doctrines of democracy he was propagating.' Is it any wonder then that this great Englishman should have been forced to spend the last decade of his life as a political exile in Pennsylvania?

People of strong moral fibre, who hold to their principles, make powerful adversaries. Like a pinch of yeast in a batch of dough their effectiveness is out of all proportion to their numbers. And so, those English dissenters who successfully withstood prolonged persecution had a powerful influence throughout society.

WA—J

Their alternative system of education had been remarkably effective; successful careers in many fields were built on this. But it did not rest there. Those who have suffered persecution and injustice themselves, will be the first to appreciate the sufferings and deprivation of others, especially their less privileged brethren. Thus it is that through the eighteenth and nineteenth centuries these people led the way, although not of course exclusively, in many areas of social reform and philanthropy, and frequently outside their own vocational sphere.

In that period when voluntary hospitals were being established in provincial towns, to replace the monastic foundations which had been swept away during the Reformation, it is interesting to discover how many of these people played a leading role, and by no means all of them medical men. Northampton,[1] which organised this service early, owed its hospital (in 1745) in part to Philip Doddridge, who would appear to have had quite enough on his plate already with his Ministry and his Academy. Later, in Newcastle-upon-Tyne,[2] Rev. William Turner was promoting smallpox vaccination, encouraging the foundation of the Medical School, was on the committee for the House of Recovery – as the early fever hospitals were euphemistically called, and engaged in other medico-social ventures besides.

In Manchester Dr. Thomas Percival was a pioneer in the field of Social Medicine.[3] In a setting where domestic and factory conditions were quite appalling his influence brought about some of the early health legislation for factories. But probably because these laws were more often honoured in the breach than in the observance his role is largely forgotten. Together with his friend and fellow student John Aikin, much was done to promote better hygiene in hospitals. Percival also put together a code of medical ethics, which is claimed in the U.S.A. as the model for the **Ethical Code of the American Medical Association.**

John Aikin advised the penal reformer John Howard on hygienic measures to lessen disease in prisons; and also assisted by editing his great publication on 'The State of the Prisons'. The long struggle of William Wilberforce for abolition of the slave trade was assisted and sustained in many ways by Aikin, Mrs. Barbauld[4] and a host of their friends.

In the field of education these people did not confine themselves to catering for their own narrow interests; they went far beyond in promoting schools, Sunday schools, Mechanics Institutes, Adult Education and libraries. The 'Warrington Circulating Library', established by John Seddon in 1758, is a good example, which forms the core of a really fine local history and reference library to this day.

For those who were already better educated they stimulated the desire for new knowledge by establishing cultural societies providing a forum for lectures and discussions. The **Manchester Literary and Philosophical Society** grew out of a series of informal meetings held in the home of Thomas Percival, who was to become its President for many years. It acquired its own building and a fine library, which sadly was destroyed in a bombing raid during the second World War. In **Newcastle-upon-Tyne** William Turner was one of the founders and first Secretary of the **Literary and Philosophical Society** there, which has an even more splendid home with a vast and valuable library still surviving. Dr. Williams's Library in London is another great repository for literature relating to the history of dissent, together with a broad selection of works on religion and education.

Although Manchester's Literary and Philosophical Society was contemporary with the Academy there, **Warrington** did not acquire its Society[5] until **1870**, more than eighty years after the Academy's demise. However, in those intervening years, there had been a succession of other more or less transient organisations culminating with the Microscopical Society, which was formally abolished to make way for the Literary and Philosophical Society, thus endeavouring to catch up with its more illustrious contemporaries. It is now Warrington's oldest society, and in excellent good health.[6]

In Politics the Dissenters were radical and liberal, loosely allied with the Whigs. Here also they were at odds with the Tory/Anglican establishment. They favoured causes such as the liberation of the American Colonies, and the Revolution in France, which made for them powerful enemies in high places at home. In view of these attitudes they had increased difficulty in attaining some of their own more immediate aspirations. The campaign for the repeal of the Test Acts, promoted by a Warrington graduate – Henry Beaufoy M.P., was thwarted on several occasions, and eventually found favour in 1828 only just before Catholic Emancipation was conceded.

Priestley, as already mentioned, was a champion of religious freedom, and wrote powerfully in opposition to Lord George Gordon's campaign which sparked off the anti-Catholic riots of 1780. He himself was a victim of the same type of bigoted mob in 1791 during the Birmingham riots. Mrs. Barbauld was another whose pen was busily engaged at the same time. She wrote a blistering pamphlet in 1790 when, yet again, repeal of the Test Acts was refused by Parliament. She was so forthright that Horace Walpole referred to her as 'That Virago Barbauld', and yet there was nothing intemperate about her language. In 1793 King George III decreed a 'Fast Day' so that the nation should mourn and do penance shortly after his brother monarch had been executed in France. Her contribution on this occasion, 'Sins of Government, Sins of the Nation',[7] exposes the cant, humbug and hypocrisy of the whole exercise as she saw it. Such refreshing candour was not welcomed.

This study, which has charted many notable achievements, is also a story of missed opportunities. The vision and enthusiasm of the 1750s was already fading by the '70s and '80s. It is an odd feature of human endeavour that having proved a certain development is possible, further growth can be adversely affected as waning interest, if not sheer apathy, succeeds enthusiasm.

Against this background the factors of weak management and ill discipline combined to bring down the Warrington Academy. Moving to Manchester revived hopes, but similar problems undermined that phase also. The long years of exile at York brought fundamental changes: strong management and a dedicated body of students made for a much healthier establishment, but it took on much more the aspect of a seminary, somewhat remote from the mainstream of evolving higher education.

Moving back to Manchester in 1840 provided fresh opportunity in a more vibrant climate, were it not for the fact that trustees were continually looking over their shoulders, towards London and Oxbridge. An enlarged, talented and broader based academic staff seemed poised to take a lead in the establishment of a University at Manchester, but this was not to be, as Owen's College grasped the baton.

After little more than a decade the decision was made to forsake Manchester and move to London, in the shadow of the new university there. But again it was out of the mainstream. There was gifted leadership by York graduates in the York tradition, but this again meant that the college was more of a seminary on the fringes, than a university college in the old Oxbridge tradition. It was in this form that the transition to Oxford was made in 1889. And so an establishment which at Warrington or Manchester might have blossomed into a major full-blown university was destined to become a subsidiary college in one of the older foundations.

Times change, and the descendants of yesterday's rebels become today's conservatives. As individuals thrive and prosper they tend to settle for ease and comfort, past disputes lose their excitement and fervour, theological controversy loses its edge; the choice for many is between apathy and a via media. The days when the establishment clergy, who were a majority on the Board of Longitude, could prevent Priestley going with Captain Cook on his Voyage of Discovery, are long since past. Education at all levels is freely accessible across the board. But is the system any better than, or even as good as, that which the Dissenter Academies provided at their best? It is at least questionable. The resources are far superior, but when computers replace brains will mankind have reverted to the status of Dean Swift's 'Yahoos'? It need not be so, but we must beware!

Warrington has been at the centre of this study of major progress in Higher Education. Its University was stillborn, so what does it have to mark its great heritage today? There is still a Priestley Street, a thoroughfare almost without houses. Off it lie the remains of Aikin Street, Howard Street, Wakefield Street and Enfield Street – presently a waste land at the rear of the District General Hospital. Priestley House is used by the Social Services and the District Education Office. This would seem appropriate, but how many who are engaged there know anything of the man? His name adorns one of the plaques on the front of the old technical college building, commemorating ten of the immortals of Philosophy and Science. But who looks up? Priestley College is for VIth form students, and wholly appropriate this should be. But, with rare exceptions, the best response to be hoped for from any student is a notion that Priestley equates with oxygen. The remainder of his career is a blank!

Barbauld Street has recently been taken out of the inner circulatory system, returning to tranquility and near anonymity; Academy Street has been widened at the expense of the last remnant of the purpose-built Academy. Holt Street and Seddon Place have disappeared from the map, and Percival Street is tucked away out of sight in Howley. Cairo Street attracts the buyer of books, and there, at least, may be some hope!

But the Academy cannot be forgotten. The recycled building at Bridgefoot adds new splendour to the town's gateway, and a generous donor has presented to the library a handsome model of the 'Stillborn University'. Such reminders may finally stir the town to a full realisation of its splendid heritage. Perhaps the time is not so far distant when the ghost of Alderman Bennett may glide through the streets of his town again, with a renewed sense of pride!

Signatures of The Warrington Tutors.

John Taylor

Joseph Priestley

G Walker

Gilbert Wakefield

John Aikin

W. Enfield

J Seddon

N Clayton

THE WARRINGTON SOCIETY
(Founded 1898)

J. HAWTHORN, Esq.
President

Dinner

to commemorate the

Bicentenary of the Warrington Academy

at the

MASONIC HALL
WARRINGTON

on

THURSDAY, 24th OCTOBER, 1957

Programme for 1957 Bicentenary Dinner – Warrington Academy

Toast List

THE QUEEN, DUKE OF LANCASTER
Proposed by the President.

THE COUNTY BOROUGH OF WARRINGTON
Proposed by C. K. SANDERS, ESQ.
(Hon. Secretary, Warrington Society)
Response by The Worshipful The Mayor
(COUNCILLOR H. G. BRANDWOOD).

THE WARRINGTON ACADEMY
Proposed by DR. J. BRONOWSKI, M.A.

PRESENTATION to DR. J. BRONOWSKI
by
The RT. HON. DR. EDITH SUMMERSKILL
Member of Parliament for Warrington

THE WARRINGTON SOCIETY
Proposed by REV. H. L. SHORT, M.A.,
Tutor and Warden, Manchester College, Oxford.
Response by the President,
JOSEPH HAWTHORN, ESQ.

RULES,

Propoſed as proper to be obſerved,

FOR THE

Better Regulation of Proceedings, in the Affair of the ACADEMY, now de ending.

I. AS the Foundation of the ACADEMY is laid in *voluntary Contributions*, it is neceſſary that the Affair be conducted with great *Prudence*; in ſuch a *fair* and *equitable* Way, as may give general Satisfaction to all Perſons concerned. Therefore,

II. The *abſent Truſtees*, who by the original Articles have a Right to vote by *Proxy*, ought not to give any Perſon, or Perſons, *diſcretionary Orders* to vote for them at the general Meetings: For, conſidering their ſuperior Numbers, this might put it into the Power of a *few* Hands to determine every thing arbitrarily in their own Way; which muſt give very great Diſguſt. Conſequently,

III. The ſaid *Truſtees* ſhould either ſend their *Inſtructions in Writing*, to be procuced by their Deputy, or Agent, at the general Meeting; or waving their Privilege of voting by Proxy, *refer* all Matters to the Deciſion of thoſe Truſtees who ſhall attend the Meeting *in Perſon*, or by their *written Orders* aforeſaid.

IV. The *Time* of every general Meeting ſhould be preciſely *fixed*, and properly *notified*, one *Month* beforehand; that ſo, if occaſion require, there may be ſufficient Time to inform the *diſtant Truſtees* of any Matters depending, and worthy of their Attention. But,

V. To avoid, as much as may be, all trout me Applications of this Kind, let the *neighbouring Truſtees* cultivate a good Underſtanding among themſelves; and endeavour, if poſſible, to agree upon all Matters of Moment in an amicable Way, before their final Determination at a general Meeting.

VI. To remove all Ground of *Emulation* between LIVERPOOL and MANCHESTER, (where it is moſtly feared) in the Choice of *Perſons* to carry on the ACADEMY; let MANCHESTER have the nomination of One, and LIVERPOOL Another, *&c.*

VII. If either Side acquieſce not in the *Nomination* made by the other, but intend to *oppoſe* it at the Time of Election; let them *notify* ſuch their Intention, one Month before the general Meeting; or, the Nomination to ſtand good.

VIII. In order to prevent all clandeſtine Proceedings, let the Committees, appointed at each Place for carrying on a fair Correſpondence, keep an exact Liſt of all the *Subſcribers* and *Benefactors*, with their Names and Places of abode; together with the Names of all *Candidates* for Offices, ready to be inſpected, by any Member of the Society, at leaſt one Month before the general Meeting: And let all Perſons, whoſe Names are not inſerted in the ſaid Liſts, be deemed incapable either of *giving*, or *receiving* a Vote, at the next enſuing Election.

IX. Let not any Views of *private Conveniency*, but a generous diſintereſted Concern for a *public* and *common Good*, be the prevailing Motive of all Meaſures and Proceedings, in this great and weighty Affair. For, this would be the Way to *conſolidate* the voluntary Aſſociation, and crown it with *Succeſs* and *Glory*.

[SADLER, Printer.]

REFERENCE ABBREVIATIONS

Ashley Smith – Ashley Smith J.W. The Birth of Modern Education (1954) London,Independent Press

Autobiog. J.P. – Autobiography of Joseph Priestley with introduction by Jack Lindsay (1970) Bath, Adams and Dart

Barbauld – The works of Anna Laetitia Barbauld with a memoir by Lucy Aikin (1825) London, Longman & Co.

Bright – Bright H.A. A Historical sketch of Warrington Academy (1858) Proc. Hist. Soc. of Lancs. and Cheshire. vol.II

Davis – Davis V.D. A History of Manchester College (1932) London, George Allen & Unwin Ltd.

Deacon – Deacon M. Philip Doddridge of Northampton (1980) Northamptonshire Libraries

Fulton – Fulton J.F. The Warrington Academy and its influence upon Medicine and Science. Bulletin of the Institute of History of Medicine. Johns Hopkins University, U.S.A. vol.1. No.2. pp.49-80

Georgian Chron. – Rodgers Betsy. A Georgian Chronicle (1958) London, Methuen & Co.Ltd.

McL. EETA – McLachlan H. English Education under the Test Acts (1931) M/c University Press

McL. W.A. – McLachlan H. Warrington Academy (1943) M/c, Chetham Soc. vol.107

Mem. J.Aikin – Aikin Lucy. Memoirs of John Aikin (1823) London, Baldwin, Craddock & Joy

Mounfield – Mounfield A. Early Warrington Nonconformity (1922) W'gton, J.Walker & Co. Ltd.

Nicholson & Axon – Nicholson F., Axon E. The Older Nonconformity in Kendal (1915) Kendal, Titus Wilson

Nuttall - Nuttall G.F. New College London and its Library (1977) London, Dr. Williams' Trust

Thorpe – Thorpe T.E. Joseph Priestley (1906) London, J.M.Dent & Co.

Turner – Turner W. The Warrington Academy (1813-15) Monthly Repository vols.8,9,10 reprinted with intr. by Carter G.A. (1957) Warrington Library and Museum Committee

W.A. Minutes – Minutes of Warrington Academy Trustees. M/c College library, Oxford (on microfilm at W'ton library)

W'gton – Warrington

M/c – Manchester

W.A. – Warrington Academy

Lit. & Phil. Soc. – Literary and Philosophical Society

REFERENCES

Chapter 2

1 Beamont Wm. The Parish Church of St. Elfin, W'gton (1878) W'gton, Percival Pearse pp.74-9
2 ibid p.75
3 ibid p.76
4 ibid p.79
5 Mounfield p.25
6 ibid p.34, also Nicholson & Axon p.218
7 ibid p.69
8 McL. EETA p.1
9 ibid p.2
10 ibid pp.45-49
11 ibid pp.6-15
12 ibid p20
13 Ashley Smith p.82
14 McL. EETA pp62-70
15 Nicholson & Axon p.116
16 Nicholson & Axon pp.113-198
17 John Cockin quoted in Brown Geo.H. (1912) Settle, The 'Caxton' Press p.3
18 Frankland R. Reflections on a letter writ by a nameless author to the Rev. clergy of both universities and on his bold reflections on the Trinity etc...(1697) London, printed for A. and J. Churchill and sold by F. Bentley, bookseller, Halifax.
19 Nicholson & Axon pp.180-7
20 Mounfield p.34
21 ibid pp.71-2
22 McL. EETA p.15
23 Mounfield pp.86-103
24 ibid p.99
25 pp.99-100
26 ibid p.92
27 ibid p.93
28 Ashley Smith pp.75-7
29 Moon N.S. Education for Ministry (1979) Bristol Baptist College.
30 Davies D.E. Hoff Ddysgedig Nyth (1976) Abertawe, Ty John Penry.
31 Orchard S. Cheshunt College (1967) Essex, Saffron Walden, Saffron Press Ltd.
32 Wadsworth K.W. Yorks. United Independent Coll.

(1954) London Independent Press Ltd. Memorial Hall, E.C.4.
33 Thompson J. Lancs. Independent Coll. (1893) M/c. J.E.Cornish.
34 Parker I. Dissenting Academies in England (1914) Cambridge Univ. Press. p.121
35 Davis pp.15-30
36 McL. W.A. pp.130-3
37 McL. EETA pp.115-7
38 ibid pp.125-6
39 McL. EETA pp.188-191 and Nicholson & Axon pp.319-29
40 Ashley Smith pp.72-3
41 ibid p.81
42 Nicholson & Axon p.315
43 ibid p.335
44 ibid p.631
45 ibid p.632
46 ibid p.630
47 ibid p.634
48 McL. EETA pp.106-9 and Ashley Smith pp.109-111
49 McL. W.A. p.133
50 Ashley Smith p.120
51 Nuttall pp.1-28
52 McL. W.A. p133
53 Ashley Smith - chart
54 McL. EETA pp.134-142 and Ashley Smith pp.111-121
55 Georgian Chron. p.17
56 Deacon pp.61-62
57 McL. EETA p.135
58 Nuttall pp.29-58
59 Ashley Smith pp.129-44 and McL. EETA pp.143-52
60 Deacon pp.100-101
61 Nicholson & Axon p.163
62 Gordon A. Addresses, Biographical and Historical (1922)London. Lindsey Press. pp.209-10
63 McL. EETA pp.21 and 146
64 ibid p.148
65 ibid p.149
66 ibid p.150
67 Correspondence and Diary of P. Doddridge (5 vols.) ed. by J.D.Humphreys, London. p.195
68 Georgian Chron. pp.28-30
69 McL. EETA pp.152-65 and Ashley Smith pp.148-52
70 McL. EETA p.163 and Williams J. Memoirs of T.Belsham (1833) London. p.398

71 Ashley Smith p.148
72 McL. EETA pp.164
73 McL. EETA p.153
74 McL. H. Cross St. Chapel in the Life of M/c. (1941) Proc. M/c. Lit. and Phil. Soc. vol.84 pp.29-41.
75 Davie, Donald A Gathered Church (1978) London. Routledge & Kegan Paul pp.67, 134-5
76 Newman John Henry The Idea of a University (1912 ed.) London. Longmans, Green & Co. Preface p.ix

Chapter 3

1 Bennett A. A Glance at some old W'gton Socs. (1906) W'gton, Mackie & Co. Ltd.
2 McL. W.A. p.11
3 Chetham's Hospital & Library, Manchester (1961) The William Morris Press Ltd.
4 Mounfield p.92
5 Crowe A.M. W'gton, Ancient & Modern (1947) W'gton, J.H.Teare & Co.
Boscow H. W'gton, A Heritage (1947) W'gton, J.H.Teare & Co.
Carter G.A. W'gton, Hundred (Part I) (1947) W'gton, Garside & Jolley Ltd
6 Sellers I. Lecture to W'gton Church History Soc. (1980) copy in public library
7 Beamont Wm. Annals of the Lords of W'gton. (1872) M/c. Chetham Soc. vols.86,87.
Beamont Wm. Annals of the Lords of W'gton and Bewsey (1873) M/c. Chas. Simms & Co.

Chapter 4

1 Gordon A. Heads of English Unitarian Hist. (1895) repro. by Cedric Chivers Ltd. Bath (1970) p.104
2 Nuttall pp.1-28
3 Turner p.3
4 McL. EETA p.145
5 McL. W.A. p.11
6 ibid p.16
7 ibid p.13
8 McL. EETA pp.16-7
9 ibid p.41
10 Jebb J. Works (3 vols.) (1787) London, Cadell, Johnson & Stockdale vol.2 p.274
11 Trevelyan G.M. Illustrated English Social Hist. London,

Reprint Soc. edn. (1963) vol.3 p.71
12 McL. W.A. pp.11-3
13 W.A. minutes - Manchester College library, Oxford
14 McL. EETA pp.280. 285-6
15 Minute book - Warrington Circulating Library from 1760. MS1 in W'gton Ref. Library
16 Burney L. Cross St. M/c and its College (1983) Didsbury, M/c. p.2
17 McL. W.A. p.14
18 Turner p.62
19 ibid p.7
20 Mounfield p.109
21 McL. W.A. pp.17-8
22 McL. W.A. pp.42-6 and Turner pp.4-5
23 Turner pp.10-11
24 Gladding Rosa E. Wesleyan Methodist Mag. 1910, March p.230
25 W.A. minutes
26 McL. W.A. p.47 and Turner pp.5-6
27 McL. W.A. pp.48-51 and Turner pp.12-23
28 McL. W.A. p.49
29 Turner pp.20-1
30 ibid p.14
31 Georgian Chron. p.46
32 McL. W.A. pp.51-59 and Turner pp.23-28
33 Autobiog. J.P. p.73
34 ibid Intro. p.12
35 Baugh A.C. (Univ. of Pennsylvania), Cable C. (Univ. of Texas) A Hist. of the English Language. (3rd edn.1976) Boston & London. Routledge & Kegan Paul. ch.9
36 Gordon A. Heads of Eng. Unitarian Hist. (1895) p.109
37 Priestley J. An Essay on the first principles of government, and on the nature of political, civil, and religious liberty (1768) London, J.Johnson
38 McL. W.A. p.55
39 Duffy E. Peter & Jack, R.Cs. and Dissent in 18th Cent. England (1982) London, Dr. Williams' Trust. p.6
40 Milburn D. A Hist. of Ushaw Coll. (1964) Ushaw p.13
41 Gillow Biographical Dictionary of English Catholics (1885) London. Burns & Oates.
42 Milburn D. Wm. Gibson, President of Douai (1957) Ushaw Mag. vol.67 pp.12,13,16
43 Priestley J. to Lindsey T. 18 Jan.1770 - original correspondence in Dr. Williams' Library
44 A Free Address to those who have petitioned for the Repeal of the late Act of Parliament in favour of the

R.Cs., by a Lover of Peace and Truth (1780) London, J.Johnson

45 Autobiog. pp.46-53

46 Priestley J. The History and Present State of Electricity (1767) London, J. Johnson printed W'gton, Eyres' Press

47 Priestley J. A Chart of History (1769) W'gton, Eyres' Press

48 Priestley J. The History and present state of Discoveries relating to Vision, Light and Colour (1772) London, J.Johnson

49 Priestley J. Electricity p.XIII

50 Gibbs F.W. Jos. Priestley, Adventurer in Science and Champion of Truth (1965) London, Nelson p.99

51 Thorpe p.216

52 Thorpe chap.IX

53 Priestley J. Experiments and Observations on Different Kinds of Air (1775-7) 3 vols. 2nd edn. (corrected) London, J.Johnson

54 Thorpe p.51

55 Kendrick J. A Morning's Ramble in Old Warrington (1855). Proc. Hist. Soc. Lancs. and Cheshire. vol.7. p.93

56 Barbauld vol.1 pp.35-38

57 'Different kinds of Air' – Priestley

58 Barbauld vol.1 pp.55-8

59 ibid vol.1 p.184

60 Catalogue of the W'gton Acad. library (1775) W'gton, Eyres' Press

61 Bright p.12

62 Georgian Chron. Letter to Dr. E. Channing. pp.52-3

63 Bright pp.14-5

64 Autobiog. J.P. pp.94-5

Chapter 5

1 Turner p.31

2 McL. W.A. p.67

3 McL. W.A. p.68-9 and Turner p.29

4 Bright p.15

5 Seddon letters. Trans. Unitarian History Soc. (1939-42) vol.VII p.280

6 McL. W.A. p.69

7 Autobiog. J.P. pp.96-7

8 Turner p.43

9 McL. W.A. pp.78-80

10 Turner – intro. by Carter p.iii

11 Turner – pp.35-40 and McL. W.A. pp.69-70

12 Mem. J. Aikin vol.1 p.296
13 Enfield Wm. The Speaker (1774) with both essays (1790) W'gton, Eyres' Press.
14 McL. W.A. p.72
15 Turner p.36
16 McL. W.A. pp.40-1
17 McL. W.A. pp.75-7, Turner pp.42-4,52, and Frankenberg R. (1963) Proc. Manchester Lit. & Phil. Soc. pp.74-93
18 Adami J.G. Chas. White of M/c (1922) Univ. Press of Liverpool Ltd.
19 Fulton pp.49-80
20 The Medical Register for the year 1779. London, J.Murray, Fleet St. pp.102-4
21 Aikin J. (1771) 'Thoughts on Hospitals' London, Joseph Johnson
22 Fulton p.68
23 Howard J. The State of the Prisons in England and Wales (1777) ed. by J. Aikin W'gton, Eyres' Press
24 Aikin J. and A.L. Miscellaneous Pieces in Prose (1773)
25 Aikin J. and A.L. Evenings at Home (1792-6) 6 vols. London J.Johnson
Note – This appeared in many editions and re-issues, for over a century, the last recorded is – Readings from . . . in 1915. (B.M. catalogue)
26 Mem. J.Aikin vol.1 pp.65-84
27 ibid vol.1 pp.174-8
28 ibid vol.1 pp.116-7
29 ibid vol.1 pp.123-9
30 ibid vol.1 pp.131-2
31 Georgian Chron. pp.112-3
32 Le Breton P.H. (ed) Memoirs, Miscellanies and Letters of Lucy Aikin (1864) pp.243-4 London, Longmans
33 McL. W.A. pp.70-2 and Turner p.42
34 McL. W.A. p.73 and Turner p.43,69
35 McL. W.A. pp.73-5 and Turner pp.43-4
36 Davie D. A Gathered Church (1978) London, Routledge & Kegan Paul. p.123
37 McL. W.A. pp.100-2 and Turner pp.44-8
38 Turner p.47
39 McL. W.A. pp.102-3

Chapter 6

1 Fulton p.51
2 Turner pp.51-79 intro. p.iii. *Note* – There are 2 lists

which do not entirely match, one of 393, the other of 402.

3 Percival E.C. The Works Literary, Moral and Medical of Thomas Percival with Memoirs of Life etc. 4 vols. (1807) London, J.Johnson also Turner pp.51-2

4 Percival T. Medical Ethics (1803) M/c, printed by S. Russell for J. Johnson

5 Leake C.D. Percival's Code (1923) Journal A.M.A. vol.81 no.5 pp.366-371

Osler W. On the library of a Medical School (1907) Bull. Johns Hopkins Hospital vol.18 no.193 pp.109-11

6 Autobiography of A.Hamilton Rowan (1840) ed. by Drummond W.H. Dublin, Thos. Tegg & Co.

Nicholson H. The Desire to Please. (story of A.H.R.) (1943) London, Constable & Co.Ltd.

7 McL. W.A. p.104

8 Bright p.23

9 Seddon letters – Trans. Unitarian Hist. Soc. (1939-42) vol.7 p.278

10 Bright p.22

11 Mem. J. Aikin vol.1 p.10

12 Barbauld vol.1 p.X

13 Thorpe p.45. *Note* – This appears to be the only instance where Anna Laetitia is referred to as Nancy.

14 Georgian Chron. p.52

15 Bright p.12

16 Ellis Grace A. Life of Mrs. Barbauld with many of her letters (1874) Boston James R. Osgood & Co. vol.1 p.43

17 Bright p.23

18 ibid p.14

19 Barbauld vol.1 pp.65-6

20 Barbauld vol.1 pp.23-8

21 Clegg's Diary ed. by Kirke (1899) Buxton, C.F.Wardlaw. 'High Peak News' office.

22 John Cockin, quoted in Brown Geo.H. (1912) Settle, The 'Caxton' Press p.3

23 Bright p.22

24 Barbauld vol.1 pp.12-22

25 Georgian Chron. pp.37-8. *Note* – When the Aikins came up from Kibworth they were advised to get their goods and chattels to Manchester, where they could be put on a barge to bring them down to the station on the Bridgewater Canal at Stockton Heath, this being preferable to the rough track from Manchester to Warrington.

26 Aikin J. A Description of the Country from 30 to 40

miles round Manchester (1795) London, J.Stockdale. *Note* – This mentions ships of 70 to 80 tons bringing goods up the Mersey which made Warrington a busy port, but smaller boats for other purposes were also to be found.

27 Barbauld vol.1 pp.168-72

Chapter 7

1 McL. W.A. pp.143-4
2 Trustees of W.A. – Annual Report – 1780
3 McL. W.A. pp.100-4
4 Mounfield p.117
5 Price E.J. Trans. Congregational History Soc. vol.II p.50
6 Priestley J.A. A History of the corruptions of Christianity (1871 edn.) sect.5 p.24
7 McL. W.A. p.102-3
8 Davis V. ch.5
9 ibid p.59
10 McL. W.A. p.104
11 Barbauld vol.1 p.262

Chapter 8

1 Davis pp.169-70
2 ibid p.54
3 McLachlan H. Cross St. Chapel in the life of M/c. (1941) Proc. M/c Lit. and Phil. Soc. vol.84 pp.29-41
Baker T. Memorials of a Dissenting Chapel (1884) M/c, Johnson & Rawson, also London, Simpkins, Marshall & Co.
4 Davis pp.54-7
5 ibid pp.63-5
6 McL. EETA pp.246-55 Ashley Smith pp.171-8
7 Parker, I. Dissenting Acadamies in England. p.136
8 Priestley, J. Heads of Lectures. p.111 note EETA p.247
9 Worthington, H. Sermon, 1789, McL. EETA p.246
10 Thorpe ch.IX
11 McL. EETA p.253
12 ibid p.254
13 Davis ch.6
14 ibid pp.84-6
15 ibid pp.92-4
16 ibid pp.88-92
17 ibid p.80
18 ibid p.101

WA—K

19 ibid p.96
20 ibid ch.7
21 ibid pp.106-7
22 ibid p.109
23 ibid pp.130-1
24 M/c Guardian. 30 March 1850
25 Davis pp.134-5
26 ibid pp.124-6
27 ibid ch.8
28 ibid p.114
29 ibid p.137
30 Drummond J. Upton C.B. The Life and Letters of James Martineau (1902) London, Jas. Nisbet & Co.Ltd. vol.1 p.263
31 Davis pp.118-20
32 Life etc. of Martineau vol.2 p.272
33 Memoir of Wm. Ellery Channing (1880) one vol. edn. Boston, Amer. Unitarian Assocn. p.435
34 Davis p.142
35 ibid p.144
36 ibid pp.155-9
37 ibid p.160
38 ibid pp.162,179
39 ibid pp.193-4
40 ibid pp.164-7
41 A short account of the Charity and Library established under the will of the late Rev. Daniel Williams, D.D. (1917) London, Dr. Williams Trust
42 Davis p.172
43 ibid p.171
44 Stuart-Page H. The most interesting house in W'gton (1898) W'gton, Sunrise Pub. Co. pp.42-7
45 Note Wm. Hamilton Drummond was also the name of James Drummond's father; he was the biographer of Archibald Hamilton Rowan.
46 Davis pp.186-7
47 ibid pp.187-8
48 ibid pp.185-6
49 Fuller A. The Calvinistic and Socinian systems examined and compared as to their Moral Tendency. (1794, 2nd edition) quoted in Georgian Chron. p.198
50 Spence-Watson, R. (1897) The History of the Lit. & Phil. Soc. of Newcastle-upon-Tyne.

Chapter 9

1 Deacon pp.119-23
2 Nicholson H.M. Trans. Unitarian Hist. Soc. vol.18 p.28
3 Hope R.B. Dr. Thomas Percival (1740-1804) M.A. thesis (1947) Univ. of M/c (copy on microfilm in W'ton Public Library)
4 Barbauld vol.1 pp.173-9
5 Bennett A. A glance at some old W'gton socs. (1905) Proc. W'gton Lit. and Phil. Soc.
6 O'Brien P. Warrington Literary & Philosophical Society (1870-1987) Lit. & Phil. Soc. (1989) W'gton
7 Barbauld vol.2 pp.379-412

INDEX OF PERSONS

GENERAL INDEX